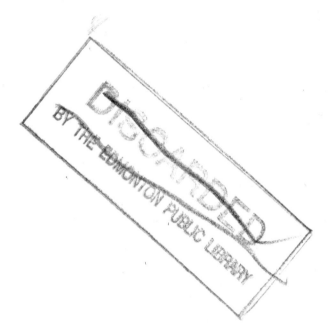

RED JENNY

A Life with Karl Marx

By the same author:

Rainer Maria Rilke

My Sister, My Spouse:
A Biography of Lou Andreas-Salomé

Zarathustra's Sister:
The Case of Elisabeth and
Friedrich Nietzsche

RED JENNY

A LIFE WITH KARL MARX

H. F. PETERS

St. Martin's Press
New York

RED JENNY. Copyright © 1986 by H. F. Peters. All rights reserved.
Printed in the United States of America. No part of this book may be
used or reproduced in any manner whatsoever without written permission
except in the case of brief quotations embodied in critical articles or
reviews. For information, address St. Martin's Press, 175 Fifth Avenue,
New York, N.Y. 10010.

Library of Congress Cataloging in Publication Data

Peters, H. F. (Heinz Frederick)
    Red Jenny.

    1. Marx, Jenny, 1814–1881.   2. Communists—
Biography.   I. Title.
HX273.7.M37P48   1987   335.4′092′4   [B]   86-24800
ISBN 0-312-00005-7

First published in Great Britain by Allen & Unwin.

First U.S. Edition

10 9 8 7 6 5 4 3 2 1

To
John and Jessie Keyser,
friends in a world of acquaintances
'magna est veritas et praevalebit'

Contents

List of Plates

Introduction

'Mrs Karl Marx, née Baroness Jenny von Westphalen' read the visiting card which Jenny had printed upon her arrival in England. But she was mistaken if she thought that she could impress the English by emphasizing her noble origin. They did not take much notice of her during her life and even later, when her husband's name had begun to reverberate around the world, hers remained but a faint echo. Yet Jenny was his wife for almost forty years and firmly believed in his message that only by establishing the dictatorship of the proletariat could the world be delivered from the curse of capitalism. She shared the misery of his refugee existence, copied his illegible manuscripts, fought off his creditors, prepared his meals and bore him seven children.

In 1843, when she married him, she was 29, four years older than Marx, but her fate had been intertwined with his long before that. She had been his play-mate when they were children, his confidante during adolescence and, after becoming secretly engaged to him, she had waited the biblical seven years to marry him. She was a vivacious and beautiful girl; many a young officer and lawyer dreamed of making her his own, but she had declined all other offers. There was only one man in her life, and she was his – for better or worse.

It has been said that behind every great man stands a woman and to understand the man you must '*cherchez la femme*'. But it is equally true that the woman behind every great man is the victim of his passions, be they for art, music, science, business or politics. Jenny was aware of that and, unlike many modern women, she was willing to accept it. 'The love of a woman', she wrote in a letter to her beloved Karl, 'is different from the love of a man and must be different'.[1] The woman, she implies, must sacrifice herself to the man. How great her sacrifice was in terms of human happiness, the reader may judge.

At the time Marx married Jenny he was on the verge of discovering the 'iron law of history', according to which the traditional division of society into masters and slaves, oppressors and oppressed, rich and poor would come to an end, because, as a result of the industrial revolution, the disparity between the wealthy and the workers had reached the point of explosion. A social revolution was bound to follow, and in order to direct the revolutionary sentiment of the masses towards the establishment of a classless society, a political party had to be founded. Communism was the instrument chosen to bring about this state of affairs. Even before he was married, Marx was committed to the concept that the law of history was as inevitable as the law of gravity: the old order would fall and communist societies would be established everywhere. His role in this preordained historic process was to arouse the workers of the world to their manifest destiny and to provide them with the intellectual weapons for the coming revolutions.

It was not to be expected that the life of a woman whose husband had set himself such a goal would be easy. Jenny worried when she heard that her fiancé was about to plunge into politics, but her love for him overcame her concerns for the future. She stood by him even in times of dire need, when she was physically and mentally sick and Marx complained about 'the perpetually weeping Jenny'. Exhausted from her hard life, she died in his arms in December 1881.

But even if she had known what lay ahead of her on that day in June 1843 when she married Marx, she would not have faltered. Marx, however, wrote to his future son-in-law, Paul Lafargue, 'You know that I have sacrificed my entire fortune to the revolutionary struggle. I do not regret it. On the contrary. I would do the same, if I had to start my career over again. But I would not marry. As far as it lies in my power I intend to save my daughter from the reefs on which her mother's life has been wrecked.'[2]

Many lives have been wrecked on the reefs of the great drama which is still going on between revolutionary Marxists and their opponents, and even in those parts of the world where communist societies have been established, the problem of 'communism with a human face' has not yet been solved. Since the communist creed is based on the inhuman concept that men are mere pawns in the historic process of materialistic determinism and that all personal aspirations, hopes and dreams must be subordinated to the collective will, a human solution is impossible.

Jenny lived and died in the vortex of her husband's fateful gospel.

1

Rebellious Blood

The circumstances surrounding Jenny's birth are mysterious. She was born in the small north German town of Salzwedel on 12 February 1814, which implies that she must have been conceived sometime in May 1813. But precisely during that period her parents were often separated as a result of the vicissitudes of the Napoleonic wars. Her father, a prominent member of the administration of Salzwedel, which was then under French jurisdiction, was arrested by the French on 1 April 1813, charged with treason and imprisoned in the fortress of Gifhorn, several hundred miles from Salzwedel. If the French kept him in Gifhorn for three months, as Jenny's East German biographer, Luise Dornemann, says, he cannot have fathered Jenny, neither before he was dragged away from his wife, as Dornemann asserts, nor upon his return. A more plausible explanation, given by Jenny's West German biographer von Krosigk, is that her father was released after three weeks, came home and stayed with his wife for about a month before he was again arrested.

Jenny's father, Ludwig von Westphalen, the youngest of four sons born to Philipp von Westphalen and his Scots wife, was a man of great human warmth, liberal disposition and literary interests, but he lacked two attributes which his own father had in abundance: will-power and resolution. In that respect Jenny was much more her grandfather's child than her father's. It was Philipp who raised a middle-class family to aristocratic rank – a fact of some significance in Jenny's biography.

Philipp's father, Isaak Christian Westphal, was a postmaster in Hanover and towards the end of his life – he died in 1753 – court postmaster in Brunswick. The name Isaak has given rise to the conjecture that Philipp's father was Jewish, although such Old Testament names as David, Jacob and Abraham were often used as first names by Christian families in Germany as elsewhere. Isaak, too, appears quite frequently as a first name, at least in England, as in Isaac Newton, Isaac Watts and others. The fact that it seems to be less frequent in Germany is no proof of Isaak Westphal's Jewish origin. It is true that all efforts to trace the family tree farther back have failed, and since the family historian, Ferdinand von Westphalen, Isaak's great-grandson, who, as Prussian Minister of the Interior, was known for his anti-Semitic sentiments, did not carry his genealogical researches beyond his great-grandfather, it has been surmised that he was afraid he might find something he would rather not know, and hence gave up the search.

Philipp was born in Blankenburg–Harz in 1724, studied law at the universities of Halle and Helmstedt and, after finishing his studies, accompanied a young nobleman on a grand tour through Europe, the traditional finishing school for the sons of the German nobility. We do not know what benefits his companion derived from this tour, but there is no doubt that it greatly enriched Philipp's inquisitive mind and increased his fluency in French, Italian and English.

On his return to Germany in 1751 he was offered the position of private secretary by Duke Ferdinand of Brunswick–Wolfenbüttel, a general in the Prussian army and only three years Philipp's senior. The official relationship between the two young men soon ripened into friendship. Ferdinand considered Philipp his *alter ego*, entrusted him with his personal correspondence, his finances and the running of the ducal household, while he went fox-hunting in England or on military missions to Prussia. He was related to the royal families of both countries and esteemed by both for his character and his courage. The outbreak of the Seven Years' War in 1756 provided Ferdinand with the chance to prove his military powers and Philipp to display an extraordinary talent for planning and preparing military operations.

The Seven Years' War has been called the first world war. Although its major theatre of operations was Europe, significant battles were fought elsewhere, since the two colonial powers, England and France, were pitted against each other. However, the cause of the war was not the ancient enmity of those two powers, but an act of aggression by the King of Prussia, Frederick the Great. He writes in his memoirs that ambition, interest, and the desire of making people talk about him caused him to decide for war. It was a desperate gamble, for he faced a coalition of the major European powers: Austria, France and Russia. Only England was on his side and supported him with money and men.

At the outbreak of the war, Duke Ferdinand of Brunswick, Frederick's only German ally, was put in command of the combined troops of England, Hanover, Brunswick, Hesse and Saxe–Gotha, an army of some 50,000 men. His orders were to keep the French in check, while Frederick fought the Austrians and Russians; a formidable assignment, because the French army was more than twice the size of Ferdinand's and led by such illustrious commanders as the Duke of Richelieu and Marshal Broglie. But Ferdinand rose to the challenge. By inspiring his soldiers through his personal example of courage in the field, he won a series of brilliant battles and kept the French at bay for seven years.

However, the Duke knew better than anyone that his victories on the battlefield had only been made possible by the ingenious strategic designs of his secretary, Philipp Westphalen. Every morning before Ferdinand left to join his soldiers, he found a note, prepared the night before by his secretary, with detailed suggestions about the most propitious plan of action. Hundreds of such notes, written in French, have survived and shed light on Philipp's extraordinary grasp of military matters. He suggested advances or withdrawals, decoys and follow-ups. He prepared careful analyses of the enemy's strength and weaknesses, advised the Duke when to make cavalry charges or order the infantry to advance: in short, he was Ferdinand's supreme strategist.

In addition, Philipp carried on throughout the war an extensive correspondence in the Duke's name with the Kings of Prussia and England. He kept them informed of the condition of the combined forces, requested reserves or increased financial support. Since the British were largely responsible for providing the latter, Philipp had to compose lengthy epistles to William Pitt, the British Prime Minister. It was a tedious process, demanding a great deal of diplomatic skill, for even after Pitt had recommended a requested sum, it had to be approved by parliament and paid by the Treasury. When all this had been accomplished and the British subsidies transferred to Hanover, Philipp had to fight German bureaucrats to get the monies released so that he could pay the troops. Frederick the Great, who thought that all members of the military commissariat were either idiots or scoundrels, was greatly impressed by Philipp's achievement in that field and so were the British who gave him the title of Adjutant-General and an annual pension of £200. But the British gave Philipp something far more important than money or a title: he found among them the woman of his heart.

Philipp's encounter in the middle of a bitterly fought war with Jeanie Wishart, the daughter of an Edinburgh minister of the church, is the stuff of a romantic novel. That two people of such diverse temperaments and backgrounds – a solemn, upright German approaching 40, totally committed to the conduct of the war, and a vivacious Scottish girl half his age – should have met at all sounds implausible. And yet it happened. It appears that Jeanie had come to war-torn Germany to visit her sister, who was married to General Beckwith, the commander of the British forces. During the course of her stay she learned that the liaison officer between Duke Ferdinand's German troops and the British was Ferdinand's secretary,

Philipp Westphalen, who not only spoke English well, but could explain better than anyone else what was happening in the war. At the request of his wife and her sister, General Beckwith invited Philipp to a dinner party at his headquarters. Philipp came, met Jeanie and won her heart.

But there was no time for love as long as the war continued; besides, Philipp had to get permission from Jeanie's parents to marry her. The chance to meet them came when Ferdinand sent him to England to give a war report to the British government. Philipp made use of this opportunity to go to Edinburgh and ask for Jeanie's hand. During a long talk between the future father- and son-in-law, he heard that the Wisharts were related to one of the oldest noble families in Scotland, the Earls of Argyll and Angus. The family claimed descent from the eighth Earl, who had been beheaded by James II for high treason. Although apparently unfounded, it was a claim cherished by all the Westphalens, even by Karl Marx, who often referred to it proudly: 'one of my wife's Scottish ancestors was a rebel in the war of liberation against James II and was beheaded in the market-place of Edinburgh.'[1]

It is a moot point whether Philipp was much impressed with his future wife's noble ancestry. He was a proud man. That his father had merely been a postmaster, and that, as far as he knew, none of his ancestors had any connection with the nobility, was a matter of indifference to him. What mattered was that his wife should feel at home in Germany and that he should be in a position to provide a gracious home for her. By frugal living he hoped to save enough to purchase a small estate at the end of the war, marry Jeanie and settle down as a country squire. This is precisely what he did.

The Seven Years' War ended in 1763. A year later Philipp bought an estate in Bornum in the Duchy of Brunswick. He was ennobled the same year in recognition of his war services. Thus when he married Jeanie Wishart of Pittarow in 1765 he was no longer the commoner Philipp Westphal but Baron von Westphalen. His friend and patron, Duke Ferdinand, wished him to remain in his service, but Philipp declined all positions offered to him because he had resolved to spend his life in the company of his beloved wife Jeanie, entertain her and teach her German. She learned it quickly and spoke it well, although she kept her 'delightful' Scots accent to the end of her long life. And she became reconciled to the fact that her name Jeanie was often pronounced Jenny by her German friends and acquaintances.

By all accounts it was a very happy marriage, blest by four sons, of whom the youngest, Johann Ludwig, born in 1770, appears to have been the favourite. He inherited much of his mother's charm but not enough of his father's energy and ambition. While his father's character had been moulded during the Seven Years' War, Ludwig's was severely tried by the French Revolution and its Napoleonic aftermath.

Like his brothers, Ludwig attended the Collegio Carolino in Brunswick and studied law at the University of Göttingen, although he was much more interested in the humanities. He loved Shakespeare, Dante and the French classical writers. While he was still a student, his father died, and since the family fortune was not large, he was forced to find a position as soon as he had finished his studies. He entered the civil service of his native Brunswick. In 1797 he fell in love with Lisette Veltheim, the aristocratic daughter of a big landowner and decided, 'in order to be worthy of her', to give up his career, buy an estate, largely with borrowed money, and become a gentleman-farmer.

For six years he tried to support his wife and his growing family in a profession for which he was totally unsuited. Neither his heart nor his head was in farming. He had bought Rondeshagen near Ratzeburg to please his wife, but even Lisette admitted that it had been a rash decision. Barely three years later he decided to sell it and buy a larger farm, chiefly because he hoped to make money by speculating in land. He thought he could resell the newly acquired property to a rich merchant in Hamburg. But this hope proved illusory. In 1804, his dream of being a gentleman-farmer shattered, Ludwig was forced to return to the Brunswick civil service. He had fathered four children: Ferdinand, the oldest and most prominent, in 1799; a daughter Lisette, in 1800; a son Karl, in 1803; and finally Franziska, who was born in 1807, a few months before the sudden death of his wife.

The year 1807 was traumatic not only for Ludwig von Westphalen. It was the year of Napoleon's triumph in Europe, the year of the Treaty of Tilsit which sealed the fate of Prussia and her allies. Brunswick ceased to exist as an independent Duchy and became part of a newly created political entity called the Kingdom of Westphalia headed by Napoleon's brother Jerome. This meant the end of Ludwig's civil service position. He either had to move his family and try for a post in the Prussian civil service, or stay where he was and work for the French administration. His decision to accept the position of secretary-general at the prefecture of Halberstadt under French rule, has been criticized. His father had fought the French for seven years; did he not now betray his heritage by serving them? Ludwig would probably have answered that he did it for the sake of his family, the world was in turmoil and the mood of the times was '*sauve qui peut*': every man for himself. Besides, he had the full support of his mother who shared his home and took care of the children.

There were moments when it would have been very difficult for him to cope with his conflicting duties, had it not been for his mother's sound Scots advice. In 1809, for example, when the deposed Duke Wilhelm of Brunswick marched into Halberstadt at the head of the 'black pack', a gang of armed supporters, and took possession of the town for a few days, Ludwig faced a critical situation. Presumably Jeanie told the Duke, then a rebel in his own realm, that the secretary-general of the French prefecture was out of town. Her charming Scots accent must have sounded convincing, for there is no record that Ludwig suffered any harassment from his former master. Still, he was probably relieved when he was transferred by the French to Salzwedel, a small town in North Germany, given the title of sub-prefect and ordered to reform the city government. This he did with his customary diligence and a good deal of success. Commerce and industry

flourished and the citizens of Salzwedel seemed quite happy
with him and their French King Jerome, who liked to be called
'König Lustik', king of good cheer.

For a few years Salzwedel provided an oasis of peace for
Ludwig and his family. While Prussian patriots were preparing for the war of liberation against Napoleon, he had
leisure for his literary interests, enjoyed the company of a few
devoted friends and, assisted by his mother, provided a loving
home for his four children. In 1810, a year before his mother
died, he met Caroline Heubel, 35 years old and no beauty, but
bright, warm-hearted and well-spoken. She was a typical
member of the German middle classes, industrious, resolute
and endowed with sound common sense. We do not know
how and where they met, but we know that Caroline was
awed when Baron von Westphalen, one of her native town's
most influential citizens, asked her to become his wife. She
knew that he had been a widower for five years and that he had
recently lost his mother, who had kept house for him; it was
obvious he needed a helpmate. Caroline happily accepted
Ludwig's offer of marriage: 'fate', she exclaimed, 'has given
me a husband whose greatness of mind and soul is equalled by
few men.'[2] For thirty years, until Ludwig's death in 1842, she
was his devoted wife, mother to his four children by Lisette
and to the three she bore him.

In April 1813 a small detachment of Russian Cossacks
entered Salzwedel, and as the allies of Prussia in the war
against Napoleon they were received with enthusiasm by the
populace. Even Ludwig, who had been installed in his office
by the French, paid his respects to the Russians. Marshal
Davoust, who drove the Cossacks out of town a few days
later, was informed of Westphalen's 'treason', had him
arrested and sent to Gifhorn, where he was roughly treated.
Caroline watched, almost beside herself with grief, as her
husband of only a few months was led away. She was left
alone in Salzwedel with four stepchildren and completely in
the dark as to when, if ever, she would see him again. She was
overjoyed when he returned home a few weeks later.

But Ludwig's troubles were not yet over. A few months after his return to Salzwedel Napoleon fell, the Kingdom of Westphalia was dissolved and the Duchy of Brunswick restored. Salzwedel came under Prussian jurisdiction. Sensing that a return to the civil service of his native Brunswick might be difficult because he had worked for the French, and since he liked living in his wife's native town of Salzwedel, he requested to be allowed to continue in his position as prefect in the Prussian administration. His request was granted. It was felt in Berlin that a man who had been incarcerated by the French must be a very great friend of the Prussians and deserved to keep his job.

Ludwig's life seemed, at last, to have entered a period of personal and professional calm. Caroline was an excellent stepmother and he adored the little girl she had just given him. As he watched Jenny grow he thought that she resembled his mother, not only in name but in looks. She had the delicate skin colour of the Scots, dark auburn hair, green eyes and the impish temperament of a true-born Highlander. He loved holding her in his arms, singing lullabies and telling her stories, to which she paid rapt attention. The beautiful old baroque house with its oak rafters and bay windows, where she spent her infancy, still stands in what is now called Jenny Marx Strasse. It was an ideal place for a young princess to grow up in. But alas, it all came to a sudden end.

In 1816, two years after Jenny's birth, the landed gentry of the district of Salzwedel chose to elect a prefect from their own ranks. They preferred a 'real Prussian' to a man from Brunswick who had served the French and seemed to be infected with some of the liberal ideas of the French Revolution. The authorities in Berlin bowed to the local will. They decided to transfer Ludwig von Westphalen to a city that had recently come under their jurisdiction and where a man of liberal disposition would be an asset; a city in the Rhineland and close to the French border: Trier. There Jenny grew up, went to school, made friends, learned about life, and met her fate – a boy named Karl Marx.

2

A Childhood in Trier

As non-Catholics in the largely Catholic town of Trier, the Westphalens were outsiders. However, when they arrived in 1817, Trier had been under French rule for two decades and many paid lip-service to their church while they eagerly discussed the new ideas of the French Revolution in the Casino society, a literary and social club, dedicated to free thought and revolutionary political ideas. 'We live in fateful times', Jenny's father wrote to a friend, 'a time in which two contradictory principles are at war: that of the divine right of kings and the new one which proclaims that all power belongs to the people.'[1] This war raged within Westphalen all his life. His heart was on the side of the people, but his head told him that as a Prussian civil servant he had to uphold the divine rights of his king. In his position as First Councillor in the government of Trier he was under Prussian jurisdiction, which was becoming increasingly reactionary. Promised reforms were countermanded, press censorship was tightened and the freedom of assembly restricted. Although Westphalen tried to carry out his duties within this reactionary framework, his superiors in Berlin, sensing that he did so half-heartedly, gave him only minor assignments and never promoted him. From a personal standpoint this state of affairs was actually beneficial for Westphalen, leaving him time for his family and the pursuit of his literary interests.

Trier had only some 12,000 inhabitants in 1820, but it did have an excellent theatre, where plays by Lessing and Goethe, Racine and Corneille, Marlowe and Shakespeare were regularly performed, an opera-house specializing in Mozart, and a very lively social life centring around the Casino society. First Councillor Westphalen and all the members of his family were received with open arms by Trier society, and Jenny's lifelong love for the theatre, and her delight in reciting poetry and singing were kindled here. It is true that as she grew up she noticed that not everybody in Trier enjoyed such a carefree existence. In his reports to Berlin her father frequently pointed out that there was 'great and growing poverty among the lowest classes'[2] of Trier and the surrounding countryside, but when Berlin asked him what caused it, he failed to provide an answer. Was it caused by poor harvests or by poor management, was it the result of heavy taxation imposed by the previous French administration or by the upheavals of the Napoleonic wars? Later, under the influence of her husband, Jenny would answer that there was so much poverty among the working people and peasants of her native town because they were being exploited by landowners and merchants. But that was later: while she was growing up she felt sorry for the poor, but enjoyed her own privileged position.

When Westphalen moved his family to Trier, he brought only his youngest son Karl from his first marriage. He arranged to have relatives take care of his daughters Franziska and Lisette, and left his oldest son Ferdinand in Salzwedel to finish high school and go on to university. Thus Jenny grew up without sibling rivalries. Her half-brother Karl, who was eleven years older than she, treated her kindly and helped her occasionally with her school-work. Her closest playmates were her sister Laura, born in 1817, and her brother Edgar, born two years later. After Laura's sudden death at the age of five, it was Edgar with whom Jenny shared the joys of her childhood. Of sorrows there were not many.

She knew nothing of the problems her parents faced when they had to decide where to send Jenny to school. Should a non-Catholic girl go to a Catholic school? Or should a Protestant teacher be hired to give her private lessons? The small Protestant congregation of Trier employed one teacher for more than a hundred boys and girls. It is unlikely that Westphalen would have sent Jenny there, since he would not have been very interested in having her taught Protestant doctrine. As a non-dogmatic Christian he would probably have reasoned that it would benefit Jenny most if he sent her to one of the two excellent private Catholic schools where, in addition to the basics, she would learn history, geography and French, as well as home economics and needlework: he himself would teach her about Luther and the Reformation. What was finally decided and where Jenny went to school, we do not know. We do know that she was confirmed in the Protestant faith in 1828 and that her confirmation motto was: 'Still I live, yet not I, but Christ liveth in me.'³ She said later that neither Christianity nor any religion meant anything to her, but she kept her confirmation motto written on a small slip of paper to the end of her life.

Soon after his arrival in Trier, Westphalen made the acquaintance of Heinrich Marx, one of the town's most prominent lawyers. He was born Hirschel ha-Levi Marx and he was the scion of a long line of rabbis. Early in his life he had decided not to follow in the footsteps of his ancestors, but to study law instead. Jews could only practise law in Prussia since an edict of 1812, and even then, they had to obtain official permission, which might be refused. During the reactionary period following the Napoleonic wars it was rare for a man of the Jewish faith to be allowed to practise law in Prussia or the territories under Prussian jurisdiction. Heinrich Marx tried to obtain permission to continue in his profession by addressing an appeal to the Prussian Governor-General of the Rhineland. He said it was an honour to serve the 'noblest of kings', in whose fatherly heart he put all his trust. But to no avail. The President of the Supreme Court of the Rhineland declared in 1816 that Jews were not permitted to practise law, no matter how highly respected they were by their fellow-citizens. Marx had the choice of giving up either his profession or his faith. Reluctantly, he chose the latter, for although he personally was a man of the Enlightenment and had no strong attachment to Judaism, he knew that his baptism would deeply offend his family, in particular his oldest brother Samuel, the chief rabbi of Trier. Sometime between April 1816 and August 1817, Hirschel ha-Levi Marx became a Protestant and continued to practise law as Heinrich Marx. It was at that time that he met the First Councillor of Trier, Ludwig von Westphalen.

The two men, both in their forties and both opposed to the illiberal policies of their superiors, came to know and respect each other. They were both members of the Casino society and participated in social events that were looked upon with suspicion by the Prussian authorities. It was said that at banquets, toasts were often drunk to individual members of the parliamentary assembly known as the Rhenish Diet, but none to the King and that on occasions even the Marseillaise was sung. In Berlin this would have been considered treason, but in the Rhineland people in general found it amusing.

The friendship between Westphalen and Justizrat Marx, who had been given the honourable title of 'Royal Prussian Legal Councillor' after his baptism or, as Heinrich Heine put it, after he had bought his 'entrance ticket to European culture', extended to their children but not to their wives. Marx's wife Henrietta, the daughter of a rabbi from Nimwegen in Holland, never felt at home in Germany and was ill at ease in social gatherings where the conversations touched on subjects that did not interest her or which she did not understand; she preferred to remain what God had made her: a Jewish mother devoted to her family. On the other hand, Caroline von Westphalen performed with ease and considerable tact the social duties which her newly acquired station in life demanded. Respected by her servants and supported by her husband's love, she made her home into a centre of high-spirited social life. She organized poetry readings, often inducing her husband to recite passages from his beloved Shakespeare, gave dinner parties for visiting dignitaries and encouraged her beloved daughter Jenny to present dramatic sketches as a training in self-assurance and poise. And she was at all times ready to listen to questions from her children or her stepchildren. It was her mother's example that Jenny kept in her heart all her life. That was how she wanted to bring up her children, although circumstances often prevented her from doing it.

Jenny's closest friend and confidante in a mostly very happy childhood was Sophie Marx, who was two years younger than she. She was five years old when she laid eyes on Sophie's brother Karl, then a one-year-old baby still at his mother's breast. As he grew up, Jenny realized that Karl was an extraordinarily determined human being, strong-willed and brooking no interference from anyone. 'He was a terrible tyrant; he forced them all – Jenny, her brother Edgar and Sophie – to push him in a cart fast down the Markusberg, and what was even worse, he insisted that they eat the pie he had baked with his dirty hands from even dirtier dough. They submitted to it because, as their reward, Karl told them marvellous stories.'⁴ This anecdote, told many years later by Jenny's youngest daughter Tussy, sheds light on a basic trait of Karl's character: in any group activity it was he who would assume command. Jenny was twelve at the time and Karl only eight, but she submitted to his will then, as she did later when she was his wife. And she was not the only one. Her brother Edgar, a year older than Karl, followed him blindly, first in school – they both attended the Friedrich Wilhelm Gymnasium – and later as a devoted communist. Even Jenny's father was attracted to Karl, the boy with dark searching eyes, who was so eager to learn and, quite unlike his son Edgar, asked so many intelligent questions. In long walks he opened up for Karl the worlds of his favourite poets, reciting passages from Homer, Dante and Shakespeare, and explaining that the principal theme of Goethe's *Faust*, 'striving' – 'he who never ceases striving will be redeemed'[5] – was the ultimate truth of existence.

Sometimes Jenny, then sixteen and a budding beauty, would join Karl and her father on their long walks through the countryside. Her father had taught her English and she too could recite Shakespeare, but now she learned about the French Revolution and its effects. Karl wanted to know why the Revolution had broken out and her father tried to explain that its main cause had been the callousness and indifference of the French aristocracy to the suffering of the people. Both Karl and Jenny agreed with Westphalen that such a society deserved to go under. However, her father was quick to point out that the Revolution was not the answer either, for it gave rise to a regime of Terror and to the dictatorship of Napoleon. There were better ways to alleviate suffering and bring about greater social justice. He spoke about Saint-Simon, the father of French socialism, whose ideas he shared. Society was responsible for the moral and physical condition of the poorest classes. It had to provide work and a living wage to everyone, if necessary by limiting the amount of private property and inheritance rights. It had to eliminate drones and idlers, 'social parasites', and subject the condition of society to a scientific analysis.

Such discussions made a deep impression on Karl, who called Westphalen his 'dear fatherly friend'.[6] Many years later he dedicated to him, as 'a proof of his love',[7] his first publication, his PhD thesis: 'You, my fatherly friend, have always been to me a living example that idealism is no illusion but the truth.'[8]

By the time Jenny was seventeen she had become the centre of the social whirl of Trier, the *Ballkönigin*, and was in such demand for parties, dances, picnics, sleigh-rides and excursions on the Moselle river that she temporarily lost track of her thirteen-year-old playmate Karl. She was being courted by men twice his age, young government officials, lawyers and officers, who found her charm infectious and her vivacious temperament irresistible. And she enjoyed the attentions she received. Her father watched with mixed emotions, but her mother basked in her daughter's glory. What happened next was to be expected.

After a particularly enchanting midsummer party a young lieutenant, with whom she had danced all night, fell upon his knees before her and asked her to become his wife. His first name was also Karl – Karl von Pannewitz. Jenny, carried away by her handsome suitor, accepted, and her mother lost no time in informing the family that Jenny was engaged to a young man from a very distinguished family. Her father was less enthusiastic. He remembered that the mother of his first wife Lisette was a born Pannewitz of whom he did not have very fond memories. In any case, Jenny was far too young to be tied down for life to a man at the beginning of a military career. In the months that followed Jenny's engagement became the topic of discussions, at times very animated, among all the members of her family. Most of them blamed her mother for what they considered Jenny's rash decision. She should have waited, she should have tried to get to know the young lieutenant better before accepting his proposal. Now that she had done so publicly, he would be exposed to public ridicule if she should decide to break the engagement. Everybody, except her mother, considered it a most unfortunate affair – soon even Jenny thought so too.

She discovered very quickly that while it was fun to dance and flirt with her fiancé there was nothing she could talk with him about other than matters concerning his regiment or forthcoming manoeuvres. When she questioned his insistence on discipline and obedience by quoting 'this above all, to thine own self be true', he smiled and said it was all right for a poet to say such things, but a soldier had to follow the orders of his superiors. Jenny wanted to know if he would shoot into groups of the poor protesting against their miserable conditions, as had happened in Paris in July 1830. Pannewitz shook his head sadly and said 'orders are orders'; it might be hard to follow them sometimes, but a soldier had no choice. Jenny protested vehemently. Her father had taught her that above every man-made law stood the law of one's conscience. That was true for civilians, her fiancé replied, but a soldier has sworn on oath to obey, regardless of his own feelings. She could not get this conversation out of her head and slowly her feelings began to change. A few months after she had accepted Pannewitz's proposal she told him that she could not become his wife. He was downcast but not broken-hearted. Fortunately, his regiment was ordered to leave Trier and Jenny was spared the embarrassment of subsequent social meetings.

In defiance of the criticism of some of her family, who felt that out of respect for the feelings of her ex-fiancé, she should limit her social activities, Jenny made full use of her regained freedom, went to parties and dances and celebrated her eighteenth birthday in the company of dozens of admirers. But the Pannewitz episode had taught her to be more circumspect with serious suitors.

Her father, who had been opposed to the Pannewitz affair from the beginning, welcomed her back with open arms to the free-wheeling discussions he was holding almost daily with Edgar and Karl, who were both students at the Gymnasium in Trier. Their headmaster, Hugo Wyttenberg, was a man of progressive ideas. He taught them history, emphasizing the study of contemporary events, because he was convinced that an understanding of the present was a prerequisite for an understanding of the past. The 1830s held no shortage of significant lessons. Europe was in the throes of a series of upheavals and revolutions. In Poland and Italy, France and Belgium the people were on the barricades to protest against the existing order. In Germany too there was much unrest, especially among the young. The most memorable event occurred on 27 May 1832, in the small village of Hambach in the Palatinate, where some 30,000 young Germans assembled in protest against the existing political order of their fatherland. Their battle-cry was 'unity and liberty'. The authorities' answer was to arrest the leaders and issue the Karlsbad Decrees which abolished both freedom of assembly and freedom of the press. In Prussia a witch-hunt was ordered. Police spies tried to ferret out anyone with subversive ideas. Wyttenberg was high on their list, as were Westphalen and his friend Justizrat Marx.

It was an exciting time for Jenny and her friends. They read and discussed the Hambach speeches, wished that they could have been present too, and were impatient with Westphalen's sober analysis of the events. He reminded them that it was easy to start a revolution but very difficult to establish a new and just order. They argued that the political order in Germany was antiquated and obsolete. France and England were unified countries, so why should there be dozens of principalities, dukedoms, kingdoms, and free cities in Germany? They wanted a united Germany, preferably a republic, but if it had to be a monarchy, then it should be one like England, with a constitution and a parliament. A king should serve not by the grace of God but by the will of the people. Westphalen shook his head. ' "Will of the people" is a phrase which has no meaning, even though the French now use it. Most of the people are ignorant and far too busy with their own lives to understand or care for the affairs of state. The people want *panem et circenses*, bread and circuses. A wise ruler will see that they get it.'⁹

Jenny noticed that her brother Edgar was far less eloquent in such discussions than Karl, who often presented arguments her father found hard to refute. A wise ruler, Karl retorted, must be a philosopher, according to Plato. Do you see any philosophers on German thrones? Westphalen had to agree that he did not. His superiors in Berlin were making life increasingly difficult for him and threatened to retire him four years before he had reached 65, the traditional retirement age of Prussian civil servants. The threat was not carried out, largely because there was another Westphalen in the Prussian civil service, his oldest son Ferdinand.

Unlike his father, Ferdinand enjoyed the confidence of his superiors to such an extent that they promoted him to the position of *Oberregierungsrat*, High Councillor, in Trier before he was forty, a rank which his father never attained. Since they were both working for the same administration, Ferdinand's rapid advancement must have hurt Westphalen's pride, even though he was pleased about his son's success. Ferdinand's attitude towards his father was that of a son who wants to help, but is frustrated by his father's easy-going life-style. It was all very well for businessmen and their ilk to belong to the Casino Club, but not for officials or officers. His father's friendship with the Jewish lawyer Marx was another indiscretion. Marx had been the main speaker at a banquet celebrating the Club's anniversary and had praised the King for favouring popular government, which was news to the King and led to an official investigation into both Marx's and Westphalen's loyalty to the monarchy. As if that were not bad enough, Ferdinand was outraged when he heard the rumour that his beautiful half-sister Jenny had become secretly engaged to that ne'er-do-well son of Marx, Karl.

3

Loving a Wild Boar

The die was cast in August 1836. Jenny was twenty-two years old and radiantly beautiful. She was surrounded by suitors who vied to make her their own, but she was restless and unfulfilled: the lightning of love had not struck her heart. When it did, it was for a boy she had known all her life. He had said goodbye to her in October 1835, as he left to study law at the university of Bonn. She had wished him luck and asked him to let her know how he was getting on. This he promised and promptly forgot. The student Karl Marx, emancipated from his home town, had better things to do than letter-writing. He kept even his family wondering what he was doing. In November his father wrote admonishing him: 'More than three weeks have past since you left and no word from you. You know your mother and how anxious she is. Your negligence is unpardonable! It confirms, unfortunately, the opinion I have of you, that despite your many good traits the prevailing force in your heart is egotism.'[1] We do not know what Karl answered, except that his father noted his reply was 'barely legible'[2] and that he could not make head or tail of the poem Karl had written.

Furious writing of poetry, reading and lectures on law and mythology occupied him during the day; his nights were filled with riotous partying, drunken revelry and duelling in the traditional style of a German freshman student. He had become a member of the Men of Trier Society and in a fight with a fellow-student from the Borussia Corps had cut his left eye. He had also been arrested and spent a night in jail for rowdiness and drunkenness and was accused of carrying prohibited weapons in Cologne (probably a pistol, for students were allowed only the use of foil and sabre). All these extra-curricular activities, which he carried on in the company of his fellow collegian, cost more money than his father had counted on giving him when he sent him to Bonn. To prove his needs, Karl sent his father some unpaid bills. Although Marx Senior did not understand what the bills were for, he wrote to his son: 'I note that you need money and so I am sending you 50 thalers. That, together with what you had when you left, amounts to 160 thalers. You have only been gone five months and don't say exactly what you need. I find this strange. I repeat, dear Karl, that I'll do gladly what I can; however, I am the father of many children and you know that I am not rich, hence I cannot and will not do more for you than is necessary for your well-being and your professional advancement.'[3] The quest for money, first from his father, later from his mother, his relatives, friends, party comrades and in the end from his patron, the capitalist Friedrich Engels, became a leitmotiv of Karl Marx's life. He always needed money, a lot of money, but never learning how to earn it, he devoted his life to writing about it. *Das Kapital* is the fruit of his long quest.

At the end of his freshman year in Bonn, Karl returned home and decided, after lengthy discussions with his father, that he would continue studying law at the University of Berlin. His father probably reasoned that the capital of Prussia was a more suitable environment for serious studies than a small town in the Rhineland. For his part Karl was attracted to Berlin because Hegel, one of Germany's best-known and most controversial professors of philosophy, taught there, and Karl was really much more interested in philosophy than in law.

Soon after his arrival in Trier Karl paid a visit to his friends, the Westphalens, who greeted him warmly. The Baron wanted to know what books he had read and what he thought of his professors. Edgar queried him eagerly about his fellow collegians and what the Bonn girls were like, and Jenny – Jenny just stared at him, blushing at her own feelings. He had grown a black beard and his head was crowned with a mop of black hair. His dark skin, his strong body: suddenly the picture of a black wild boar came to her mind and made her shiver. '*Schwarzwildchen*' she was to call him in her love letters, her darling little wild boar.

The first flush of their love was interrupted when Karl had to leave Trier for Berlin. Jenny felt forsaken. She needed to confide in someone, but did not dare tell her parents. Fortunately there was Sophie, Karl's sister, who was thrilled to be a go-between for them: and then there was Karl's father. He had guessed what was happening and they had confided in him. He was happy for them, but counselled caution. He did not want his friend, Baron von Westphalen, to take offence at Karl's presumption. Jenny would have to prepare her parents to accept him as their future son-in-law. And Karl would have to work hard, finish his studies and find a respectable position. 'I have talked with Jenny and wish I could calm her . . . She does not know how her parents will accept her news. And what her relatives and the rest of the world will say . . . The sacrifice she is making to you is inestimable. Woe to you, if you should ever forget it. You must now show that you are a man who deserves the respect of the world.'[4] Such admonitions Karl received from his father. His sister wrote to him: 'Jenny loves you. She worries about the difference in your ages mainly because of her parents. She is hoping to prepare them gradually and then you must write to them. They hold you in high regard.'[5] That Jenny's father liked Karl and thought he was a very bright young man, is true enough, but it took time before he could bring himself to see in him a future son-in-law. His daughter had been engaged for seven months and he knew nothing about it. 'Jenny feels very depressed that her parents know nothing, or, as I think, want to know nothing,'[6]

Marx Senior informed his son, telling him at the same time that he had gained Jenny's complete trust. 'The dear, dear girl is tormenting herself, she is afraid she is hurting you, forcing you to over-exert yourself in your studies.'[7]

Karl's answers were couched in phrases of poetic extravagance: 'A new world arose for me when I left you, the world of love, hopeless love at first, but drunk with longing. Even the journey to Berlin which otherwise would have enchanted me and aroused my interest in nature and my love of life, left me cold; indeed, it depressed me, for the rocks I saw were not steeper or bolder than the feelings of my soul, the busy cities not busier than my blood, the meals in the inn no more overloaded and indigestible than the creation of my fancy and finally, art not as beautiful as Jenny.'[8] He devoted his first months in Berlin to love and poetry. As a present for Christmas in 1836 he sent his fiancée three collections of his poems. The first was entitled *Book of Songs*, the second and third *Book of Love* and all three were dedicated to 'my dear, eternally beloved Jenny von Westphalen'. His sister wrote to him: 'Jenny was visiting us yesterday and wept when she received your poems, tears of joy and sorrow.'[9] Jenny loved poetry and it moved her deeply to hold in her hands three volumes of poems written for her by the man she loved. Although Marx later dismissed these poems as youthful indiscretions, an opinion shared by most Marx scholars, they shed light not only on an early phase of his life, but provide deep and often disturbing insights into the working of his mind; thus he writes at that time in *Oulanem. A Tragedy*:

> And we are chained, shattered, empty, frightened,
> Eternally chained to this marble block of Being,
> Chained, eternally chained, eternally.
> And the worlds drag us with them on their rounds,
> Howling their songs of death, and we —
> We are the apes of a cold God.[10]

Commenting on these lines, Robert Payne says: 'the annihilating judgment, visited on the world and on men, was never far from Marx's thought. He had little pity for the world or for the men who crawled on its surface, those "apes of a cold God", eternally in bondage.'[11] But for Jenny these poems conveyed only Karl's youthful passion, expressed in the style of the German Romantic poets. At the same time as she was moved she worried that she might not be able to keep her ardent young lover: 'What makes me so miserable, dear Karl, is precisely that which would fill the hearts of every other girl with bliss: your beautiful, moving, passionate love, the incredible beautiful way in which you express it, the passionate pictures of your fancy – all these cause me great anxiety and often despair . . . my fate would be terrible if your ardent love were to cease.'[12] Such thoughts puzzled Karl, for had he not told her:

> See: I could a thousand volumes fill,
>   Writing only 'Jenny' in each line,
> Still they would a world of thought conceal,
> Deed eternal and unchanging Will,
> Verses sweet that yearning gently still,
>   All the glow and all the Aether's shine
> Anguished sorrow's pain and joy divine,
>   All of Life and Knowledge that is mine.
> I can read it in the stars up yonder,
>   From the Zephyr it returns to me,
> From the being of the wild waves' thunder.
> Truly, I would write it down as one refrain,
>   For the coming centuries to see –
> LOVE IS JENNY, JENNY IS LOVE'S NAME.[13]

He had become a member of the Doctors' Club, a circle of young men in Berlin who spent endless hours debating Hegel's philosophy. They met in the 'red room' in the Café Stehely on the Gendarmenmarkt, read newspapers, drank beer and sparred words. One of their members was Bruno Bauer, a young radical theologian who criticized the Gospels, claimed that they were without historical significance and preached a revolution in Christianity. He became Marx's mentor and, since he held a lectureship at the University of

Berlin and later in Bonn, encouraged Marx to prepare himself for a similar position. His father did the same. He advised his son to work steadily, make friends with influential people in Berlin and try his hand at writing a play or an ode with a patriotic theme honouring Prussia and the genius of monarchy, perhaps evoking the spirit of the noble Queen Louise. If he succeeded, his name would become known and his chances of getting a professorship improve. Karl was a voracious reader and he wrote furiously, ream after ream, taking extracts from books, penning aphorisms, writing essays and poetry, but his father's idea that he write an ode in honour of Prussia made him laugh. He wanted to be free and in Prussia the laws and restrictions left him a slave. He was appalled by the idea that he might have to serve in the Prussian military for a year. When he was drafted in February 1838, he asked his parents to send him a certificate stating he was medically unfit to serve. His mother did so, because his father was too ill to write: he died on 10 May 1838, while Karl was in Berlin.

Karl had been in Trier at the beginning of May for a few days, had seen his father and Jenny, who wrote to him after his father's death that she was deeply distraught because he had called her a 'mean girl'[14] during a lovers' quarrel. 'My heart stopped; you realized what you had done and begged me for forgiveness. You did so in a moment of ardent love, but what can I expect once your heart is cold? Oh, Karl, this thought is hell.'[15]

Jenny was not the only one who had forebodings about the future. In letter after letter his father had expressed misgivings about his son's character. 'Thoughts of you and your future uplift my heart, and yet I cannot rid myself of sad and terrifying ideas that enter me like lightning: is your heart equal to your head, is it capable of gentler feelings?[16] . . . You are dominated by a demon not given to everyone, is this demon divine or Faustian? Will you ever be – and this is the most painful doubt in my heart – will you ever be receptive to truly human, domestic happiness?'[17]

Most members of Jenny's family shared these doubts. When her half-brother Ferdinand, who had become First Councillor

in Trier, learned that his beautiful sister was engaged to Karl
Marx, he requested the Berlin police to keep him informed
about the activities of his future brother-in-law. He was
alarmed by what he learned. Marx was not a serious student of
law at all. He was attending classes in philosophy and history,
but wasted most of his time arguing about God, Man and
Society in the company of young radicals and atheists, while
consuming beer and wine by the litre and smoking black
cigars. Ferdinand communicated this news to their father and
insisted that Jenny be forced to break her engagement. But
while Baron von Westphalen agreed that Jenny had acted
rashly, he did not feel he should or could interfere with her life.
She was twenty-four years old and strong-willed. And perhaps Karl would settle down after sowing his wild oats in
Berlin. Ferdinand disagreed. He told his father it was his
responsibility to protect the well-being of his children. He
should warn Jenny that he would disinherit her if she did not
break her engagement.

Jenny, having her own doubts about the future, became ill
and left her native town at various times, keeping in touch
with her fiancé by mail. Some of these letters have survived
and their tenor is always the same: passionate and eternal love.
And always her worry: will he remain true to her? 'My
darling, my dear and only darling, please write to me soon and
tell me that you are well and that you still love me.'[18]

Undoubtedly Karl tried to reassure her of his devotion,
although he met many women, some of them famous, during
his five student years in Berlin. It is said that he frequented the
literary salon of Bettina von Arnim, a leading member of the
circle of Germany's young romantic poets. Karl was attracted
to Bettina, who was more than thirty years older than he, not
only because she spoke eloquently about Goethe, whom she
had met as a child, but because of her concern for the conditions of the poor. Poetry and social questions – these were the
two main topics that interested him. Much to Jenny's chagrin
he invited Bettina to come to Trier with him. One of Jenny's
schoolfriends, Betty Lucas, remembers:

I entered Jenny's room one evening, quickly and without knock-ing, and saw in the semi-darkness a small figure crouching on a sofa, with her feet up and her knees in her hands, resembling more a bundle than a human figure, and even today, ten years later, I understand my disappointment when this creature, gliding from the sofa, was introduced to me as Bettina von Arnim . . . the only words her celebrated mouth uttered were complaints about the heat. Then Marx entered the room and she asked him in no uncertain tone to accompany her to the Rheingrafenstein, which he did, although it was already nine o'clock and it would take an hour to get to the rock. With a sad glance at his fiancée he followed the famous woman.[19]

Jenny was upset but forgave him as she always did, then and later. 'I hope you behaved yourself on the Rhine steamer or was there another Madame Hermann on board? Oh, you wicked rascal. I shall cure you of that. All these steamship trips. Such wanderings I shall lay under an interdict in the *"contrat social"*, our marriage contract, and all such abnor-malities will be punished verbally. I shall specify all cases and demand atonement; I shall institute a second, severe common law; a marital law. Just you wait. I shall get you.'[20] The banter-ing tone of this passage from a letter to her beloved little wild boar is revealing. She was concerned about his fidelity and had a right to be, although, unlike his friend Engels, Marx was no philanderer. He merely seized the occasion for sex with other women when it was offered him.

From one of Jenny's letters it appears that they had sexual relations some two years before they were married. She wrote to him from Neuss, a little town on the left bank of the Rhine opposite Düsseldorf, where she had gone to visit friends and get away from her family. Karl was in Bonn hoping to get a professorship. Jenny planned to visit him on her way back to Trier, but had been given strict instructions by her mother that she was to do so only in the company of her brother Edgar. Engaged couples could only see each other in the presence of a chaperon. Her mother reminded her that for the sake of 'outer and inner decency' she must not violate this rule. In her letter to Karl Jenny confesses that her mother's admonition had placed a heavy burden of guilt on her soul. 'Outer and inner decency!! – alas my Karl, my sweet and only Karl! And yet, Karl, I cannot feel any repentence. I close my eyes and see your blessedly smiling eyes and rejoice in the thought that I have been everything to you, that I can be nothing to anyone else. Oh, Karl, I know very well what I have done and how the world would dishonour me, I know it, I know it – and yet I am blissfully happy and would not surrender the remembrance of those hours for any treasure in the whole world.'[21] The thought of what people in her home town would say about her if they knew what she had done, made her shudder. 'My parents live there, my old parents who love you so much; oh Karl, I am bad, I am very bad and nothing is good in me except my love for you . . . The end of your love would be the end of my life. And there is no resurrection after such a death.'[22]

The recipient of such passionate epistles of love was still at loggerheads with himself over his professional future. He had been at the University of Berlin for five years and had no diploma or degree to show for it. His mother urged him in vain to graduate and get a position. He preferred reading, writing bits and pieces of satirical prose and poetry and arguing with fellow-members of the Doctors' Club. They considered him a brilliant, if wild and unruly, fellow whose very appearance commanded attention; an impression which is reflected in the following lines of a poem written by Bruno Bauer's brother Edgar:

> Who comes rushing in, impetuous and wild –
> Dark fellow from Trier, in fury raging,
> Nor walks nor skips, but leaps upon his prey
> In tearing rage, as one who leaps to grasp
> Broad spaces of the sky and drag them down to earth,
> Stretching his arms wide open to the heavens.
> His evil fist is clenched, he roars interminably
> As though ten thousand devils had him by the hair.[23]

The worst of those ten thousand devils, thought Marx, was

his mother, who held the purse strings. To pacify her and because he knew that a degree would help him get started in life either as a professor, a writer or a journalist, he sat down and wrote a doctoral dissertation on 'The Difference between the Democritean and Epicurean Philosophy of Nature'. His thesis foreshadows his later dictum: 'The philosophers have only *interpreted* the world, the time has come to *change* it.'[24] He submitted his dissertation not to the University of Berlin, where he was registered, but to the University of Jena, which he had never attended. Jena conferred doctoral degrees to students *in absentia* without requiring examinations and without inquiring into a candidate's personal or professional opinions. His dissertation was promptly accepted and the degree of Doctor of Philosophy conferred upon him in April 1841.

With this entrance ticket to an academic career in his pocket, he travelled to Bonn, hoping to get a lectureship there, although he also toyed with the idea of becoming a journalist. By way of introducing 'Dr Marx' to his friends in the Rhineland, Moses Hess, who had met him at the Doctors' Club, wrote:

> You will be delighted to meet a man who is one of our friends here, though he now lives in Bonn, where he will shortly become a lecturer. He is a phenomenon who has made a tremendous impression on me, although my interests lie in an entirely different direction. In short, you can look forward to meeting the greatest, perhaps the *only real philosopher* now living. Soon, when he makes his *debut* (both as a writer and as the incumbent of an academic chair) he will draw the eyes of all Germany upon himself wherever he may appear in public, whether in print or on the rostrum. Dr Marx, as my idol is called, is still quite a young man (aged about 24 at the most) and will give medieval religion and politics their final blow. He combines a biting wit with deeply serious philosophical thinking. Imagine Rousseau, Voltaire, Holbach, Lessing, Heine and Hegel united in one person, I say united, not lumped together – and you have Dr Marx.[25]

A few months after he had penned this grandiloquent

description of the young Marx, Moses Hess, the son of a
wealthy Rhenish industrialist, further expressed his admiration by inviting Marx to join him and Bruno Bauer on the
editorial board of a newly founded liberal newspaper, the
Rheinische Zeitung. Jenny, who had hoped that Karl would
find an academic berth and at last be in a position to marry
her, was alarmed; 'Oh, my dear, dear darling, now you even
start meddling in politics. That is the most daredevil undertaking. Remember, Karlchen, that you have a sweetheart at
home who hopes and cries and is entirely dependent on your
fate.'[26]

These were difficult years for her. She was 28, still one of the
prettiest girls in Trier, but most of her girlfriends had long
since married, her brother Edgar had left home and she was
still waiting for her union with the man she loved. It was little
comfort to her that he could visit her more often now and
show how passionately he loved her. She had already become,
and perhaps a little too much, his 'wifey', she wanted to be
his wife. 'Tell me, Karlchen, that I shall soon be yours
completely.'[27]

Compounding her worries was her father's failing health.
He was the only person in the family with whom she could
talk freely about her love for Karl and her hopes of becoming
his wife. Karl had dispelled the Baron's original misgivings by
dedicating his doctoral dissertation to him. When her father
died in March 1842, her half-brother Ferdinand became head
of the family and Jenny shuddered at the thought of how he
would react if he knew how intimate she had been with her
fiancé. Fortunately her mother agreed that nobody could or
should stop Jenny from becoming Karl's wife. To make things
easier for all concerned she moved from her home in Trier to a
smaller house in Kreuznach, a resort in the Palatinate. There,
far from the gossips of Trier, she and Jenny watched Karl's
unfolding career as a journalist.

Karl's income as an occasional correspondent of the
Rheinische Zeitung was not sufficient to support himself, let
alone a wife. He had been in Trier pleading with his mother

to let him have his share of his father's estate, but to no avail. Henriette reminded him that his father had wanted him to become a lawyer, not a freelance journalist, and she was not going to finance a way of life of which his father would strongly disapprove. Marx felt frustrated and outraged. When his friend Arnold Ruge chided him for not having sent a promised article, he exploded and said that he had not been able to work for weeks because he had been involved in a most unsavoury family quarrel. 'Although my family is well-to-do, it is placing such obstacles in my way that I am at the moment in the direst straits. I cannot possibly bother you with an account of these private scandals, since fortunately public scandals prevent a man of character from being bothered by private ones.'[28] The public scandal which was bothering Marx at the beginning of his career as a journalist was the issue of press censorship.

In his first political article, published on 5 May 1842, Marx argued for an inalienable human right: freedom of expression. This article, and five that were to follow, was written in answer to a debate going on in the Rhenish Diet about freedom of the press. Marx insisted that there must be no interference by any governmental agency with the free expression of ideas. 'A free press is a mirror that presents the truth, however unpleasant it may be; a censored press is a distorting mirror and hides the truth.'[29] Written in a calm and graceful style, these articles on censorship have been numbered among Marx's most brilliant works. Ironically, they could not be published in any totalitarian state today.

Deeply impressed by both the content and the style of Karl's articles, Jenny wrote him that a terrifying thought had struck her some time ago, the thought that he had lost his right hand in a duel. She was terrified and yet happy, for 'darling, I thought I could then become really indispensable to you; then you would always love me and keep me. I thought that I could then write down all your heavenly thoughts and be really useful to you.'[30] Marx never lost his right hand, but his handwriting became so illegible that he needed Jenny to copy all his manuscripts. At this time he was both his own writer and editor. Jenny was overjoyed when he told her in October 1842 that he had become editor-in-chief of the *Rheinische Zeitung* and had been promised an annual salary of 600 thalers. At long last their future together seemed secure.

4

A Bookworm's Honeymoon

The young editor-in-chief of the *Rheinische Zeitung*, a news-paper financed by a group of Rhineland industrialists, kept his fiancée in Kreuznach informed how he was getting on in Cologne by sending her daily articles he or his associates had written. Jenny felt that he was now really in his element. He wrote to her that he was engaged in a war on two fronts – one against the Prussian censor, an idiot who crossed out every-thing he did not understand – thus he had crossed out a remark about Dante's *Divine Comedy* by declaring that in Prussia the divine could not be treated as comedy – and the other against his radical Berlin friends who tried to spread communist ideas in book reviews and essays. 'I declare that I consider it improper, indeed immoral, to smuggle into casual reviews of plays communistic or socialistic dogmas, hence a new world view. If communism is to be discussed I demand a different and far more thorough treatment of it.'[1] Thus Marx to his friend Ruge on 30 November 1842.

Jenny remembered that in her discussions with Karl and with her father the question was often raised as to what a society should do to help the poor. Her father insisted the best method was Christian charity, although a group of contemporary French writers demanded that the state should put limits on private property and prevent the amassing of great wealth. Proudhon's famous dictum 'property is theft' was heatedly discussed. While she and Karl thought the world would be a better place if there was only common and no private property, her father explained that the idea of common property was by no means a new idea, early Christian sects had lived by it and it was the life style of monks and nuns even today. However, the ordinary mortal was no saint and it was a natural human instinct to acquire property. It would require force to compel a man to give up his property – force or faith in a communist society.

Jenny was glad that Karl did not allow his friends to use his paper for the propagation of their radical ideas. What mattered was that under Karl's editorship the number of readers of the *Rheinische Zeitung* was increasing steadily. She was proud and happy when he wrote to her a few weeks before Christmas that his paper now had 3,000 subscribers compared with 1,000 in October. Everybody agreed, even those members of her family who were very critical of Karl, that it was a considerable achievement to have made a national organ from a small local paper in a few months. Her faith in him was completely justified.

While she and her mother made preparations for a quiet Christmas to which Karl was invited, she received a series of articles he had written in answer to a debate in the Diet concerning wood thefts. They were sharper in tone and more polemical than his previous articles and treated a theme that was heatedly debated. Karl criticized the Diet for having just passed a law forbidding the gathering of branches from the forests. The law had been issued because some great landowners had complained that not only dead twigs and branches were taken but often entire trees. They demanded, and the new law concurred with them, that anybody who was found in a forest with branches or twigs should be arrested and condemned to pay a fine. The new law was resented and resisted by many people. The peasants declared that it had been their God-given right from time immemorial to collect berries, mushrooms and twigs in their native forests. They gave vent to their feelings in violent tavern debates and mass meetings. The young editor Karl Marx considered it only right and proper for the *Rheinische Zeitung* to become a mouthpiece for the popular indignation. In a series of brilliantly written articles he declared that according to tradition and natural law, branches and twigs on the floor of the forest belonged to the poor and not to the landlords. Wood falling from trees was common property, just as the rain would be. Jenny felt that Karl had written these articles entirely in the spirit of her father and rejoiced with her mother when she noticed how great an interest they aroused. She did not know that the Prussian censor was not at all pleased with what were called 'polemic pamphlets', and Berlin decided to watch the young editor more carefully.

In the months that followed, Marx played a cat-and-mouse game with a number of Berlin censors. When it was suggested that the *Rheinische Zeitung* should change its tendency and assume one more in favour of Prussian policies, he wrote a long letter to the Royal Prussian Chief of Censorship, Eduard von Schaper, in Koblenz in which he declared that 'the *Rheinische Zeitung* will also in future, as far as it can, pave the path towards progress, in which Prussia leads the rest of Germany.'[2] And he rejected forcefully the reproach that the *Rheinische Zeitung* was 'propagating French ideas and sympathies in the Rhineland.'[3] He declared that it was the main task of his paper 'to concentrate our gaze on Germany and promote a German liberalism in place of a French liberalism; this surely cannot be disagreeable to the government of Frederick William IV.'[4]

It may be doubted whether such arguments impressed the Prussian officials who hated the very concept of liberalism, regardless of which flag it sailed under. Their suspicions concerning the intentions and mentality of the editor of the *Rheinische Zeitung* increased in consequence of the publication of a series of articles about the distress of the Moselle vintners. As a result of the German Customs Union, which had been established under the leadership of Prussia, it was becoming increasingly difficult for the wine-growers between Trier and Koblenz to maintain themselves against the competitions of cheaper wines from southern Germany. Marx had heard that the Prussian censor had suppressed an official complaint by the mayors of the cities concerned and published it in the *Rheinische Zeitung*: 'The country along the Moselle between Trier and Koblenz, between the Eifel and Hunsrück, is very poor because it lives exclusively from growing wine; the commercial treaties with Germany have given this industry a death blow.'[5] These articles caused an outrage in Berlin. Marx was instructed to prove his assertions or else he and his paper would have to take the consequences.

Jenny and her mother noticed that Karl was obviously worried about the future of the *Rheinische Zeitung* during the few days at Christmas he spent with them in Kreuznach. He had just heard that as a result of Prussian pressure, a Saxon newspaper, the *Leipziger Allgemeine Zeitung*, had been forced to suspend publication and he wondered whether his paper would suffer a similar fate. Jenny assured him she would stand by him whatever happened and gave him daily proof of her passionate devotion. 'If only I could smooth all your paths',[6] she wrote to him, 'if only I could remove everything that stands in your way. But alas it is not our lot to control the wheels of fate. We have been condemned to passivity from the Fall, from Madame Eve's offence. Waiting, hoping, enduring, suffering is our lot'.[7] Her most ardent wish was for Karl soon to become her 'legal, altar-worthy little husband.'[8] In their talks during the Christmas holidays in 1842 they agreed to hold the wedding in June 1843.

Soon after his return to Cologne Marx made the acquaintance of a censor who had been sent from Berlin specifically to watch over him and his paper. His name was Wilhelm Saint-Paul and he was a smart cultured cynic. In long and witty conversations he tried to convince the young editor that the nice-sounding slogan of the French revolution – *Liberté, Egalité, Fraternité* – could not be taken seriously by any thinking person, whereas the Prussian ideals of Right, Law and Order were acknowledged by everyone as natural laws. Saint-Paul had been ordered to persuade Marx to give up his editorship in Cologne, come to Berlin and enter Prussia's civil service, since his father had also been a Royal Prussian Councillor of Justice. In the course of their conversations Saint-Paul insisted that service was a higher ideal than freedom. The motto of Frederick the Great was 'I am the first servant of my people', and Goethe, whom Marx admired, had said: 'Man is not born to be free and there is no greater happiness than serving a prince, whom one respects.'[9]

The idea of serving the King of Prussia seemed absurd to Marx. Did Saint-Paul not realize that the age of monarchy was over, that the world was moved by revolutionary ideas and that in Germany and France the bourgeoisie would come to power and proclaim a republic? From such conversations with the young editor of the *Rheinische Zeitung*, the censor concluded that Marx could not be dissuaded from his liberal ideas and that the only way of preventing him from spreading them was either to remove him from his position or to suppress the paper.

The Prussian authorities had in 1842 granted the *Rheinische Zeitung* a licence to publish, because the old and respected *Kölnische Zeitung* was obviously an organ of the Catholic Church. Berlin hoped that the new paper would serve the Protestant cause in the Rhineland. This was particularly important because Protestant Prussia wanted to prevent a recurrence of what had happened to the Kingdom of the United Netherlands in 1830, when the Catholics of Belgium had risen against their Protestant masters and seceded from the Netherlands. Among the Catholic population of the Rhineland a powerful anti-Prussian sentiment prevailed, caused not only by religious differences but by different life-styles. In the eyes of the happy-go-lucky Rhinelanders the Prussians were dull law-and-order types, always ready to stand at attention.

The *Rheinische Zeitung* did not provide its Catholic readers with much to be grateful for, but it soon was a thorn in the eyes of its Prussian censors:

It committed its greatest crime – according to Prussian opinion – in January 1843 by publishing a markedly anti-Russian article. It held the despotism of the Czar responsible for the miserable life of the Russian people, the serfdom of the peasants and for the official and ecclesiastical corruption. The article caused dismay in Berlin, in St Petersburg anger. Since friendship with Russia had been an important element of Prussian policy from the time of Napoleon, Berlin waited anxiously to see what kind of reaction the 'malicious piece in the *Rheinische Zeitung*' would provoke in its powerful neighbour. The die was cast on 8 January when the Prussian Ambassador to the Court of St Petersburg was severely reprimanded by Czar Nicholas I during a conversation at a ball in the Winter Palace and ordered to stop the infamous liberal press of Germany. In reply, the three Prussian ministers responsible for press censorship decided to revoke the publishing licence of the *Rheinische Zeitung* as of 31 March 1843.

This order led to noisy protest meetings in many parts of Germany, especially by young people who considered the *Rheinische Zeitung* the most significant champion of their hopes and wishes. Petitions were presented in Cologne, Aachen, Elberfeld, Düsseldorf, Koblenz and Trier demanding that the prohibition be rescinded. For Jenny they were exciting weeks. Her beloved wild boar was being hailed as the champion of the ideal of freedom of thought, and although she realized her economic future would be precarious should he lose his fight, she assured him again and again that he could count on her whatever happened. Even if he had no job and no chance of getting one, she was determined to become his wife in June. In the meantime she collected signatures and asked all her friends and relatives to protest against the prohibition of the *Rheinische Zeitung*.

But Karl was sick of the eternal battle with the censor. In a desperate attempt to save the paper, if not his position, he raised an accusation against himself in an article published anonymously in the *Mannheimer Abendzeitung*. He wrote that 'Dr Marx is solely responsible for the sharp criticism and the truly brilliant dialectics with which the empty words of the representatives of the Diet were reported and reduced to absurdity.'[10] But the ironic expression 'solely responsible' did not appeal to the Berlin censors. They insisted on their order that the paper would have to cease publication. On 17 March, the *Rheinische Zeitung* published a brief announcement: 'The undersigned declares that he has left the editorial office of the *Rheinische Zeitung* as of today on account of the present conditions of censorship. Cologne on 17 March 1843. Dr Marx.'[11]

Jenny had hoped that Karl would win his fight with the censor, but when he sent her the brief announcement of his resignation, she said proudly to her mother that Karl had the courage to condemn publicly Prussia's hated reactionary system which her half-brother Ferdinand praised and supported. She was convinced the people of the Rhineland would understand and appreciate Karl's action. When her mother wanted to know what Karl now intended to do, she told her that he and his friend Arnold Ruge planned to publish a journal outside Germany, in order to provide uncensored expression for all opinions. Karl had mentioned Zürich, Strasburg, Brussels or Paris as possible locations for such a journal. Jenny was ready to follow him wherever he wanted to go, but she made no secret of the fact that she was worried about the future. 'Last night some ideas occurred to me concerning Strasburg. Would it not become difficult for you to come back home, if you betray Germany to France in that manner?'[12] Karl did not have such thoughts; on the contrary, he was ashamed of being a German. He wrote to her that during a journey to Holland a short time ago, he had experienced how disapprovingly people talked about Germany whose 'despotism stands in all its nakedness before the eyes of all the world'.[13] He considered it an honourable task to put an end to this despotism, a task he was not going to shirk.

Categorically he informed his friend Ruge: 'The fate we are facing is the coming revolution.'[14]

But first of all he wanted to marry. He assured Ruge, with whom he was going to publish in Paris the *Deutsch–Französische Jahrbücher*, as they had decided to call their anti-establishment journal, that he had been engaged for more than seven years and that he

> was in love, absolutely, with heart and soul, and my bride had fought the hardest fights for me, fights that have undermined her health, partly against her pietistic–aristocratic relatives to whom the Lord in Heaven and the Lord in Berlin are equal objects of veneration, partly against my own family where some priests and other enemies of mine have installed themselves. I and my bride have therefore had to fight for years more unnecessary and injuring fights than many others who are three times older and constantly talk about their 'experience of life' . . .[15]

Marx travelled to Kreuznach, where he was received by Jenny with open arms. She had asked him not to bring any presents but to save money for their honeymoon. Should he want to bring her flowers, then they ought to be pink coloured, for 'they would be best for my green dress. But I would really prefer it, if you did not bring anything'.[16] She made preparations for a civil marriage as well as for one in a church. But she insisted that before getting married 'a marriage contract between Karl Marx and Jenny von Westphalen'[17] should be drawn up which declared in the first article that there should be community of property between the couple, with the exception of the agreed clause in the third article; 'Every marriage partner should pay the debts he has made, contracted, inherited or otherwise incurred before the marriage; hence these debts are excluded from the community property.'[18]

The modern reader may wonder why a young woman of the 19th century would order a Royal Prussian lawyer to draw up a marriage contract, and even more why Marx signed it. It is said that Jenny was a business-like woman who knew that

Karl had the habit of incurring debts, particularly since his mother refused to pay his paternal inheritance. However, it is more likely that the marriage contract with the debt clause was concluded upon the urging of her mother and her half-brother, who thought that, having failed to prevent the marriage, they should at least protect Jenny from her fiancé's existing debts. In the end Marx's signature turned out to have been a pure formality, for all her life Jenny had to fight against her husband's creditors.

The marriage between Dr Karl Marx, domicile Cologne, and Miss Johanna Bertha Julie Jenny von Westphalen, domicile Kreuznach, took place on 19 June 1843 in the Paulskirche of Kreuznach, although Marx was even then an atheist. Only Jenny's mother, her brother Edgar and some friends were present; nobody from Karl's family. After a short honeymoon journey along the Rhine, the young couple took up residence in the house of Jenny's mother in Kreuznach. Caroline returned to Trier with Edgar.

Jenny and Karl planned to stay about a month in Kreuznach and then go somewhere abroad. Their destination depended on negotiations that Ruge was conducting with Fröel, the publisher of 'democratic periodicals', and with a number of friends who were supposed to finance the enterprise. These negotiations dragged on month after month and Jenny soon noticed that the honeymoon bedroom was turning into her husband's study. He had brought with him some twenty-four works in forty-five volumes dealing with French, English, German and American history and he was studying them carefully. Jenny was surprised by the numerous notes he took. He made notes from almost every page, and his notebook from the time of their Kreuznach honeymoon comprises 250 pages. Sometimes Jenny wondered whether she had married a man or a bookworm, but because she loved him, she made sure that his reading time was uninterrupted. And Karl acquainted her with a world he was just discovering, a world beyond the selfish competitive struggle of bourgeois society, a world of social justice and human dignity.

He read to her extracts from an essay on which he was working, about the emancipation of the Jews. It was a critical response to an article by his former friend Bruno Bauer, entitled 'The Jewish Question'. Bauer's argument was that basically the question of the emancipation of the Jews was a religious question and could only be solved if the Jews were willing to give up their religion. But Marx, whose father had done precisely that, did not accept this argument: 'let us consider the real, secular Jew, not the Sabbath Jew as Bauer does, but the everyday Jew. What is the worldly base of Judaism? Material necessity, self-interest. What is the object of the Jew's worship in this world? Usury. What is his worldly god? Money.'[19]

It is unlikely that Jenny wondered why the son of an old Jewish family passed such a harsh judgment on his Jewish fellow-citizens, first because she never doubted his intellectual superiority and then too because she knew how much he resented it that his Jewish mother did not hand over his inheritance. If money was the god of the Jews, then Karl was entitled to condemn them, just as he was right to call the struggle for money the curse of bourgeois society. Unfortunately, their future depended on a solution to the question of where the money would come from so that they could leave Germany and establish their own household. As months passed without an answer to that question and Jenny discovered that she was pregnant, her worries increased. She was therefore greatly relieved when, in the middle of October, Ruge informed them that the financial problems of the *Deutsch–Französische Jahrbücher* had been solved and that as a co-editor Marx would receive a salary of 1,800 francs a year.

Joyfully Jenny packed her few personal belongings, bade farewell to her mother and travelled to Paris, 'the new capital of the new world'.[20]

5

The Clarion Call of the Gallic Cock[1]

In the autumn of 1843 when Jenny and Karl came to Paris, the capital of the French Revolution, the city was a place of refuge for thousands of their countrymen and many thousands of other foreigners – Poles, Italians, Russians, Spaniards – who had either been driven out of their homelands or had left them in protest against the prevailing economic or political conditions. They came to Paris, the centre of revolutionary ideas that aroused the youth of Europe at the beginning of the 19th century and which their rulers tried to suppress by any means. Youthful radicals met in the cafés and pubs on the left bank of the Seine, the Bohemian quarter of Paris, hatched plots against their oppressors at home, founded secret societies and published pamphlets proclaiming the collapse of the existing order and the development of new forms of social life.

Marx's friend, Arnold Ruge, the co-editor of the *Deutsch–Französische Jahrbücher*, proposed setting up a communal household with Karl and Jenny, the poet Georg Herwegh and his wife Emma and another couple with two children 'for we can live more cheaply, if we can manage this ménage, i.e. a bit of communism'.[2] But Herwegh's wife, the daughter of a rich

Berlin banker, declined to participate in such an experiment. She wanted to establish her own salon, where literary and political questions could be discussed in a comfortable environment, for, like her husband, she was of the opinion that one need not give up a bourgeois life-style, even if you preach revolution. Besides, she did not think that 'Ruge's nice little Saxon wife could possibly live together with the highly intelligent and very ambitious Mrs Marx.'[3] But Karl and Jenny accepted Ruge's proposal and moved into the house he had rented in rue Vanneau, a street where the upper-middle class of St Germain lived. However, they soon realized that it had been a mistake. Life in a commune was fine in theory but less satisfactory in practice. You never felt really at home because there was always somebody else present. Jenny thought that Mrs Ruge was awfully boring and the latter considered Mrs Marx arrogant. After barely a fortnight their experiment with communism was quietly given up. Ruge, who was fifteen years older than Marx, fell ill and moved out with his wife. Karl and Jenny remained in rue Vanneau, which was also the street containing the office of the periodical which was now to be edited solely by Marx.

Paris and the Parisians fascinated Jenny. For the first time in her life she was in a capital city; all the German towns she knew were provincial by comparison. Inquisitive as she was, she spent the first weeks of her life in Paris exploring the boulevards. She admired the elegant carriages and even more elegant clothes of the ladies and gentlemen sitting in them. Her frequent companion during her stroll through Paris was Emma Herwegh who had opened her literary salon, for which Jenny envied her, and where she and Karl spent many evenings in stimulating conversation.

Herwegh, a good-looking young man about Karl's age, had become famous almost over night for a small volume of revolutionary poems entitled *Poems of One Alive*. His book was devoured by youthful readers, although – or perhaps because – it was prohibited in Prussia. Herwegh, a national hero of German youth, was invited to give poetry readings, which he did very successfully. His reading tour became a triumphal march through Germany; he was acclaimed as 'The Matador of 1842'[4] and when he came to Cologne, Marx paid him his respects.

In view of the war that he and his ministers were waging against revolutionary youth, King Frederick William IV of Prussia was so much surprised by the success of a volume of poems, that he invited Herwegh to come to Potsdam for a personal interview. That the King granted an audience to an author, whose book was banned in Prussia, 'was an event that aroused all classes of society'.[5] The King's ministers were appalled and Herwegh's friends feared that he might betray the cause of democracy. According to the newspapers the meeting was 'a sensation'. It is said that the King opened the audience with praise of Herwegh's poetic talent, adding, however, that he hoped the young poet would in future write his verses not against but in favour of the monarchy. In the expectation of being able to transform the republican Saul into a monarchical Paul, the King declared: 'I wish you from the depth of my heart a day of Damascus and your influence will be enormous'.[6] But in vain. 'I am by nature a republican',[7] was the poet's answer and to his fiancée he wrote: 'I have become much prouder after my visit to the King . . . The monarchy is dead, stone-dead for me, and has no more magic power for the world. How small, how very small and ordinary the man seemed to me.'[8] Angered by the young man's contempt for King and Country, Frederick William ordered that Herwegh be expelled from Prussia and also undertook the necessary steps to obtain Herwegh's expulsion from Saxony and Switzerland (of which Herwegh was a citizen). Like most refugees he enjoyed life in 'the new capital of the new world'[9] to the full and continued writing revolutionary poems. His ambition was to become the author of the German Marseillaise.

The fashionable life-style of the Herweghs impressed both Jenny and Karl, while Ruge was outraged by their extravagance. It was disgusting that Herwegh bought his wife expensive gowns and bouquets of flowers, wore a new pair of gloves every day, drank champagne, ate caviare and had as his mistress Comtesse d'Agoult, 'a person of the most ordinary kind',[10] Franz Liszt's mistress of many years and mother of Cosima, later the wife of Richard Wagner.

Herwegh's extra-marital affairs displeased Jenny, although she admitted that it was a male privilege to have a mistress. However, when he tried to seduce her one evening, she put him severely in his place. She hated the concepts like 'free love' and 'communalization of women' that many young radicals advocated, and although she was often tempted, she remained faithful to her husband. However, neither she nor Karl could stop spending money. The Ruges were horrified when they heard that Jenny had bought Karl a horse-whip for his birthday, which was the more stupid since 'the poor man can neither ride nor does he have a horse'.[11]

The temptation to spend money in Paris was indeed considerable. During the reign of the Citizen King Louis Philippe, whose motto was '*enrichissez-vous*', the affluence of the French bourgeoisie increased very rapidly and was ostentatiously shown off – at balls and the opera, in grand carriages on the Champs-Elysées or on horseback in the Bois de Boulogne – while the workers in the Faubourg Saint-Antoine often had to beg for a piece of bread. Marx could not afford such luxury and he reached the conviction at this time, perhaps partly from envy, partly from anger, that the bourgeoisie as a class had to be destroyed. The time was ripe for a revolution of the havenots – he called them the proletariat – against their oppressors. While other social reformers, many still Marx's friends at that time, had come to the conclusion that one must help the poor out of genuine sympathy for their sufferings, the source of Marx's bitter hostility towards the bourgeoisie was not so much pity for the poor as hatred of the rich.

Jenny did not hate the rich, she only hated being poor and hoped all her life that her beloved Karl would succeed in obtaining the means for the bourgeois life-style she was used to. They were not poor during the first year of their exile in

Paris. Karl had a solid position as the editor of a new periodical, the organ of the most progressive ideas of German and
French writers, a position at which she was convinced that he
would excel, for he had been a brilliant editor of the *Rheinische
Zeitung*. Jenny was proud to see how in their Parisian conversations, he always played the major role. It amused her to
watch him jump from his chair and, after drawing on his cigar,
reduce the arguments of the Russian nihilist Mikhail Bakunin
to a pulp, or answer quietly the reasoned objections made by
another Russian friend, Pavel Annenkov. Annenkov describes
the young Marx as a man of considerable energy, will-power
and unshakable conviction, whose sharp voice had a metallic
ring that did not permit any objection. 'In front of my eyes
stood the embodiment of a democratic dictator, as we see him
in moments of fantasy.'[12] In front of Jenny's eyes stood the
man she loved, whose child she was carrying and whose ideas
she admired. To be sure, there were moments when she
wished he would answer his political opponents in a less biting
tone and she often advised him to write less irritably, but she
never doubted that he was the prophet of a new world order.

The poet Heinrich Heine, the most prominent of the
Germans living in Paris, was also of the opinion that Marx had
come to the French capital to prophesy the coming 'world
revolution'. Heine, twenty years older than Marx, had been in
Paris for ten years because, like Marx, he wanted to express
himself without having to ask a censor's permission. The
poetry of this 'last knight of the Romantics' was so imbued
with socio-critical thoughts that the youth of Germany read it
with enthusiasm, and in 1835 the Bundestag had ordered a
prohibition of Heine's writings, published or unpublished,
prose or poetry. The effect of this prohibition was that Heine's
fame as the German poet-in-exile grew steadily and surrounded him with the aura of an unofficial poet laureate.

Marx had read Heine eagerly when he was a student and
wrote poetry. His love poems for Jenny are typical of the
Romantic flood of emotions in Heine's style that animated
young Germans at the time. What Marx's poems lacked was

the subtly ironic innuendo that distinguishes Heine's poetry. Marx may have felt it himself and given up writing poetry in consequence. But he treasured Heine's friendship and tried to strengthen it by encouraging the poet to play a more active role in the coming revolution. While he was writing his article about Hegel's philosophy of law for the *Deutsch–Französische Jahrbücher*, he remembered a passage in Heine's essay about Börne concerning religion: 'Heaven was invented for people to whom the earth has nothing to offer . . . Hail to this invention! Hail to a religion that offers suffering human kind in the bitter cup of life a few sweet, sleep-producing drops, mental opium, a few drops of love, hope and charity'.[13] Marx felt that here was the image he needed: religion was 'the opium of the people'. Heine would have chuckled if he had been told that he was the father of a communist catch-phrase. He thought it strange that his young friend Marx, who had a very attractive young wife and obviously enjoyed his bourgeois life-style, was so determined to prove that it was condemned to destruction. He asked himself what would happen, if the proletariat, as Marx called the workers, were to gain power. The thought 'the future belongs to the communists'[14] worried him, for, if they should ever obtain power 'those dismal iconoclasts, they will smash with their brutal fists all the marble statues of my beloved world of art'.[15] Marx shrugged his shoulders. It was not art that occupied him, but the concept of capital. He asked Heine to write a poem against the re-actionary Prussian regime for the *Jahrbücher*. Heine agreed, not only because of his friendship for Marx, but because he was very fond of his young wife. It was indeed in the best tradition of German Romantic poetry that a German baroness followed the man she loved into exile.

These first months in Paris were unforgettable for Jenny. It was exciting to be courted not only by the famous poet but by many other men – she mentions Herwegh, Ruge, Bakunin, Annenkov and '*tutti quanti*'. There was much talk and a great deal of typically German quarrelling: 'much gossip *à querelles allemandes*'.[16] And at the centre of it was her Karl, who was busy giving the finishing touches to the first volume of the *Jahrbücher*, which appeared in February 1844, chiefly written by Marx himself. It contained his essay 'On the Jewish Question' that he had written in Kreuznach soon after his marriage, and his critique of Hegel's philosophy of law. Heine contributed three satirical odes on King Ludwig of Bavaria, Herwegh a few poems. There was also a review of Carlyle's *Past and Present*, entitled 'The Condition of England'. Its author was a young German living in Manchester, who was to play a major role in the lives of Karl and Jenny – Friedrich Engels.

It would soon become apparent, however, that Marx had deceived himself when he thought that the *Jahrbücher* would become a regular organ for the views of the young in Germany and France. Nor would Jenny's hopes that the *Jahrbücher* would provide a steady source of income be realized. For one thing because there was not a single contribution from a French author in the first, and as it turned out the only, edition of the *Jahrbücher*. Marx had failed to obtain anything from his French friends. But above all it was crippled by a ban on the *Jahrbücher* in Prussia. In an official edict the Prussian government had declared that Marx, Ruge, Heine, Herwegh and others were traitors, accused them of *lèse-majesté* and ordered their arrest should they enter Prussia. Copies of the forbidden periodical were confiscated at the border. Moreover Ruge, named as co-editor even though illness had prevented him from doing any work for it, was horrified by what he read. He considered Marx's doctrine that the proletariat was destined to deliver mankind from the curse of private property, unfounded and offensive and refused to have anything further to do with the periodical. He even refused to pay Marx his promised salary. He said that Marx could keep the 1,000 copies owing to him and could try to sell them.

This cynical suggestion confirmed Marx's suspicion that Ruge was at bottom a bourgeois philistine who had no understanding or sympathy for the coming revolution. Jenny shared his opinion and called Ruge an 'ass',[17] whose stupid little

Saxon wife she had always disliked. That he refused to pay
Karl for his work proved to her that Ruge was not only a
philistine but malicious. Fortunately there were others who
thought more highly of Karl's struggle for a better world.
When their Cologne friends heard what had happened in Paris
they took up a collection that produced 1,300 thalers, a sum
that arrived just in time, for Jenny was in the eighth month of
pregnancy.

Her child, a girl they named Jenny, was born in Paris on 1
May 1844 – a day that half a century later would obtain a
symbolic significance, as in 1889 the First of May was declared an official holiday for the workers of the world. Jenny,
called Jennychen by her parents, had inherited from her
Scottish great-grandmother not only her name but her white,
delicate complexion, though unfortunately not her robust
health. During the first weeks after her birth her parents
worried greatly about her. Jenny could not nurse her. Apparently, Jennychen often suffered from stomach pains.
According to an often repeated anecdote which, if not true, is
ben trovato, Jennychen suffered one of her stomach cramps
while Heine was visiting her parents. Her parents watched her
writhing with pain, obviously very anxious but not knowing
what to do. Heine, on the other hand, said without hesitation:
'she needs a bath', made one and put Jennychen into it. The
baby recovered immediately and Jenny and Karl believed all
their lives that Heine had saved their child from death.

This incident and others caused Jenny to come to the
conclusion that she needed the help of her mother to keep her
beloved baby alive. She left Paris and her husband in the
middle of June and travelled with 'my mortally sick child'[18] to
Trier. Her lonely mother received her with tears of joy. She
worried much about her two children – Edgar, who had still
not finished his law studies – and Jenny, whose husband
obviously could not find a secure position. Jenny's mother
thought that now that Karl was a father, he should give up his
political agitation and try to get a regular income. Secretly,
Jenny agreed and in her letters to Karl she often expressed her

worries about the future. To her mother and her acquaintances in Trier, however, she gave the impression of being a very happy wife and mother. Admittedly, Karl did not have a secure position, but he was one of the best-known and best-hated of German journalists, and, after all, she had not come home to defend Karl against his bourgeois critics. She needed help for Jennychen who was daily becoming weaker. The diagnosis of their family doctor, to whom her mother took her, was that the baby could not tolerate the milk it got. Since Jenny did not want to suckle it herself (ladies of her class did not normally do so) the doctor proposed employing a wet nurse. Jenny disliked this suggestion, being reluctant to entrust the life of her baby to another woman. Then it occurred to her mother that Gretchen, a young girl of the neighbourhood, had just had a baby and would surely be willing to nurse Jennychen, too. Upon her mother's advice Jenny got in touch with Gretchen and heard that the young girl was not only willing to nurse Jennychen but come to Paris with her and help with the household. She had been at home hardly a week and had already found a nurse for her child that would probably have died in Paris.

She wrote Karl from Trier that he would hardly recognize her, 'unless her little eyes and shock of black hair gave her away. Everything else is really totally different, only her resemblance to you is becoming increasingly obvious'.[19] She was looking forward to a reunion after such a long separation, but had 'in the back of her mind a sombre sense of anxiety, of fear, of the threats of unfaithfulness, of the seductions and allurements of Paris'.[20]

Her friends and acquaintances in Trier watched her with curiosity, and she did her best to dress herself in elegant Parisian style in order to show the good burgers of her native town what it meant to be the wife of a revolutionary writer. 'I do not have to make any calls, everybody is coming to see me, I am being courted from morning to evening . . . and I have never in my life looked as radiant'.[21] Even Karl's mother had received her with open arms, although Jenny had been afraid to visit the old lady with whom Karl had a feud because of his father's inheritance. She asked herself why Mrs Marx, who never bothered to answer her son's letters, had taken the trouble to visit her. She answered by explaining: 'Success . . . or in our case, the *appearance* of success that I know to give by using the subtlest tactics.'[22] Jenny did not know, when she wrote those words that as the wife of the chief ideologist of the world communist movement, it would remain her task all her life to give the appearance of success. She pretended to be a good middle-class housewife even at times when she did not have enough bread for her children. It seemed important to her, if only to prove to her reactionary, but well-situated half-sisters in Berlin, that she had made the right decision when she married Karl. They did not know, poor fools, what Karl knew, namely that the ground upon which they stood would soon be rocked by a social earthquake that would destroy their temples and shops. Signs of the coming revolution were everywhere. Jenny was still in Trier, when the Silesian weavers went to the barricades in protest against their oppressors, demanding better pay and shorter working-hours. This uprising was crushed by Prussian soldiers on the orders of King Frederick William IV: dozens of workers were killed and many wounded. The paternal image of the King, propagated so persistently, was badly damaged by these events, for it had suddenly become obvious that Prussia's celebrated 'Law and Order Society' was based upon brute force.

It was therefore not surprising that a few weeks later an attempt was made on the King's life. At the beginning of August 1844 – Jenny had already been in Trier for six weeks – she received a letter from Karl which she answered at once, for the bells were ringing, the cannons firing and the pious running to church 'to sing hallelujah to the Lord in Heaven for having so miraculously saved our Lord on Earth'.[23] The former mayor of a small Silesian town, whose request for a position in the Prussian civil service had been rejected, had fired two shots at the King without hitting him. Jenny asked sarcastically: 'Did not your Prussian heart tremble with horror when you heard the news of the outrage, that scandalous, incredible outrage?'[24] She then examined the reasons for the attempted assassination. People are glad in Prussia, she writes, that the reason for the deed was not political fanaticism. 'They console themselves with *that* thought – more power to them – for here is precisely a proof once again that a political revolution in Germany is impossible, but all seeds have been sown for a social one . . . That man spent three days in Berlin begging for bread and constantly in danger of dying from starvation – hence a social attempt of murder! If it gets started it will start here, for this is the most sensitive spot, even a German heart is vulnerable here!'[25]

Marx found Jenny's arguments so convincing that he gave her letter to the editor of *Vorwärts*, a German paper in Paris, which published it with the heading 'Letter of a German Lady'. It was Jenny's first publication for her husband's cause; as he had put it in the *Jahrbücher*: 'the Clarion Call of the Gallic Cock will announce Germany's Day of Resurrection.'[26]

During the summer months that Jenny spent with her mother in Trier her thoughts were often with Karl. She wanted to know what he was doing and when she should come back to him. What she needed above all was his assurance that he was able to provide for her financially, their baby and a nurse. She wrote to him: 'I know it is bad and stupid to torture myself with all kinds of worries and forebodings, I feel it very well in those moments of self-torture – however, the spirit is willing but the flesh is weak – and I can only banish those demons with your help.'[27] In her dark forebodings about the future Karl's letters provided the only ray of hope. And he wrote to her often. He told her that he was now working for the *Vorwärts* and also assisting with the publication of a great new poem by Heine, *Germany. A Winter's Tale*, which, he was sure, she would love reading. Heine was at present in Hamburg, 'to hand over the poem, in the presence of his publisher, to the supervising officials with particular care.'[28] He had told Marx that he would bring to Paris the beginning of the book, which consists only of romances and ballads 'that your wife will like'²⁹; 'I am looking forward to seeing her soon again. I hope the coming winter will be less melancholic for us than the last one.'³⁰ Jenny hoped so too, for the time had come to forget the sorry affair with Ruge and the *Jahrbücher*. Karl wrote to her that his first article for the *Vorwärts* was an adversely critical review of an article that Ruge had written for the *Vorwärts* under the pseudonym 'a Prussian'. He had made fun of Ruge's stylistic and grammatical nonsense; thank God, they were rid of Ruge.

Another worry that Jenny shared with her mother during the months of her stay in Trier, was her brother Edgar. He was a student in Bonn, but instead of attending lectures and preparing himself for the state exam he wasted his mother's money in evenings in taverns and on visits to the opera in Cologne. To his mother he wrote that he was looking forward to the coming revolution and the complete overthrow of the existing order. Jenny's opinion was that he should not wait for the overthrow of the existing order, but that he should overthrow his own disorder. Her mother made angry remarks about the crazy, revolutionary youth of Germany. Jenny was on the horns of a dilemma, on the one hand because she was married to one of those crazy revolutionaries, on the other because she had to blame her brother for sharing Karl's ideas. Should she wait for Edgar's return from Bonn and talk with him seriously about his duties towards his mother and his fiancée Lina Schöler, or should she return to Karl in Paris? She was longing for her husband but afraid of the everyday problems she had to face. However, when Karl wrote and told her how much he missed her she decided at the end of September to leave Trier and return to Paris.

The result of their passionate reunion was what Jenny both hoped for and feared: 'Karlchen, how long will our little doll play a solo part? I fear, I fear that when Mama and Papa are together again, sharing community property, they will soon perform a duet'.³¹ As she rightly anticipated, she was pregnant again at the end of the year. Karl, who loved children, was delighted, for although he was an atheist he believed in the biblical saying: 'They do not sow, neither do they reap and yet the Lord feedeth them.' Jenny would have preferred a human breadwinner for her children, but Karl's firm conviction that the Gallic Cock would soon announce a new order of society, allayed her fears. He told her that Engels, who for almost two years had examined the condition of the working class in England, was convinced that there would soon be an uprising against the capitalistic oppressor. That would be the signal for the outbreak of socialist revolutions in France and Germany. In their struggle against their masters the workers needed intellectual leaders, a function that he and Engels could perform.

Jenny had not yet set eyes on Engels, but after her return to Paris his name was constantly on Karl's lips. Engels' father was apparently a typical bourgeois who owned cotton mills in Barmen and Manchester. Engels had grown up in the house of a wealthy and pious Rhineland industrialist and was shocked when he saw how the workers had to live under his father's employment. Men, women and children worked twelve to fourteen hours a day for starvation wages, lived in pigsties always with the fear of not having a job at all the next day. With his father's permission, Engels had gone to Manchester to see how the condition of the workers stood in the world's most advanced industrial country. What he saw outraged him. The slums in Manchester, where the workers had to live amidst garbage and disease, were appalling. Children of 8 had to work ten hours a day. The women, forced to work in sweatshops, were at the mercy of their male supervisors and syphilis was widespread.

Karl told Jenny that as a result of his observations in England, Engels had arrived at the same conclusions as he had through his philosophic investigations: the time was ripe for a revolutionary overthrow of the existing social order. The victims of that order, the industrial proletariat, would have to be convinced that the system, by which they were exploited, was not only made by men but could be changed by men. It was necessary to forge the intellectual weapons of the coming

revolutions for the workers. In England Engels had established relations with the Chartists, a group of highly moti-
vated social reformers, and he had gone home to incite the
workers in the Rhineland against their oppressors. He had
asked that Marx should do the same among the German
workers in Paris.

Marx had agreed, although he would have preferred to
write about the historically inevitable collapse of bourgeois
society. He had already taken part, together with Jenny, in
meetings of the League of the Just, a secret society of German
artisans in Paris, whose leader, August Wilhelm Weitling, a
German tailor, had aroused a considerable sensation with his
pamphlet *Guarantees of Harmony and Freedom* advocating a
primitive Christian communism. Marx called it 'the brilliant
literary debut of the German workers'.[32] Jenny, however, felt
that most members of the League – tailors, shoemakers,
carpenters, masons – looked upon Karl with suspicion. Was he
really on their side or merely a journalist in search of a good
story? Or perhaps even a police spy? She was relieved when
Karl assured her that he had no intention of becoming a member of the League or of any other secret society because he
considered the communism they preached a utopian mixture
of Christian charity and blind force. They did not know that
even a revolution must be orchestrated scientifically. Small
groups of conspirators working underground could never
force the ruling bourgeoisie to give up their power. It was
necessary to appeal to the workers and convince them that
they were the masters of their fates. That was precisely what
Engels was trying to do in the Rhineland.

Karl showed Jenny a letter he had just received from
Barmen. Engels wrote that he had to settle a love affair first
and also work on his book concerning the conditions of the
workers in England, but that he had already spoken at public
meetings proposing the establishment of co-operatives for the
improvement of the living conditions of the workers. He had
been amazingly successful. Among the workers of Elberfeld
and Wuppertal communism was becoming very popular, and

'in Barmen the commissioner of police is a communist.'[33] Marx considered these developments a confirmation of his theory and Jenny rejoiced with him. They advised their French communist friends to be prepared for the coming event, for *ex oriente lux* – perhaps their light would also come from the east.

But her joy was short-lived. The Prussian police had watched the meetings in the Rhineland, where communism was publicly proclaimed, had decided to prohibit them and to arrest the speakers. Since many of the most dangerous communistic ideas – such as the demand for revolution, regicide, atheism, and the abolition of private property – were preached in Paris by people like Marx, Hess, Herwegh and others, who tried to seduce good German journeymen, Berlin decided to request that King Louis Philippe expel these communist conspirators from France. For this reason the well-known German natural scientist Alexander von Humboldt, whom the King held in high regard, was dispatched to Paris in January 1845. He presented the King with a beautiful vase and a personal letter from King Frederick William IV with the request that Louis Philippe purge his capital of the infamous German atheists. The latter assured von Humboldt that he would be glad to do it.

While the victims of this expulsion order believed they were completely safe, prime minister Guizot was undertaking the necessary steps to carry it out. Jenny writes that in the middle of the night in January a superintendent of police appeared unexpectedly with the order: 'Karl Marx has to leave Paris within 24 hours.'[34] In reality, however, it was not necessary to obey this order unconditionally. The persons affected by it could lodge an appeal and stay in Paris, provided they abstained from any public demonstration against a friendly government. Marx did not appeal against the order and left Paris by coach at the beginning of February. Most of the other recipients of the expulsion order remained.

Jenny too had to remain in Paris for a time to break up their household, to discuss with their landlord the termination of their rental contract and to pay their debts. This meant a wearisome running back and forth in Paris, then in the grip of a freezing winter; moreover, she had to ask her friends to babysit for Jennychen, since her servant and nurse Gretchen was no longer with her, and, what was most difficult of all, she had to get the money for her own departure by selling their furniture. Karl had left her 200 francs for the landlord, but to her dismay she heard that they owed him 380 francs and that he would pay back 180 francs only after he had found another tenant. In a letter written in French to her husband, who had gone to Brussels, Jenny confessed that she did not know what she should do. 'This morning I have been running all over Paris. The mint office was closed and I have to go back once more. Then I went to the stage-coach office and to the auctioneeer of a public furniture sale. But in vain. All this running around has been useless.'[35] But Jenny was a resolute woman and not easily discouraged. Since she spoke French well, she succeeded in settling their affairs in less than a week. She spent her last two nights in Paris with the Herweghs, who had also received an expulsion order but preferred to stay in their comfortable Parisian home.

It was a sad farewell for Jenny. She had come to Paris with great expectations, convinced that her husband's cause was just and would triumph. But once again his enemies had proved stronger. The French government was no better than the Prussian. She felt disgusted by the meanness of Guizot and Humboldt. And their Parisian friends who pretended to support Karl's cause – had they not all betrayed him? Well, she would be faithful to him! 'I was sick and it was bitterly cold when I followed Karl to Brussels at the beginning of February.'[36]

6

Exile in Brussels

The first months in Brussels were just as difficult for Jenny as the last days in Paris. When she arrived in the Belgian capital after a long and tiresome journey in the coach, she found Karl in a hotel with the ominous name 'Au Bois Sauvage' in which she and Jennychen now had to live too, since there was no money for a home of their own. However, the main reason for her worries about the future was that it was by no means certain that the Belgian government would permit Karl to stay in Brussels. A German expelled from Paris because of communist activities had to reckon with being expelled from other countries at the request of the Prussian police. In order to be allowed to stay, Marx addressed a petition to the Belgian King in February 1845 humbly requesting to be permitted to stay in Belgium with his wife and child. He was granted permission only after making a statutory declaration that he would abstain from any political activity. This put a stop to his work as a journalist and a source of income.

In his distress Marx turned to his young friend Engels in Barmen who immediately sent him 50 thalers which he had 'borrowed from his old man'. Moreover, he took a collection for the Marx family among the communists in the Rhineland which produced 750 thalers and told Marx that he could count on the royalties of his newly published book *The Condition of the Working Classes in England.* This solved the problems of rent and daily bread for the time being and Jenny found a small house in the rue d'Alliance, a working-class neighbourhood in the Faubourg St Louvain.

While Jenny was still trying to get used to life in the 'pauper colony', as she called her Brussels domicile, two events occurred that would decisively influence her and Karl's life: the arrival of Helene Demuth and Friedrich Engels.

Helene, or Lenchen, as she was called, did not come to Jenny as a stranger. She had been for years her mother's faithful maid and had shared like a sister the bitter-sweet secret of Jenny's love for Karl. It had been Lenchen who had eagerly taken care of the wedding preparations in Kreuznach and had followed Jenny's life with sympathetic concern. Jenny's mother considered Lenchen not as a maid but as a member of the family. When she heard about the difficult conditions under which her daughter with little Jennychen had to live in Brussels she sent her 'the best that I can send you, my dear faithful Lenchen'.[1] It was God's gift in the truest sense of the phrase, for without Lenchen's help the Marx family would hardly have been able to weather the difficult years of exile. She stayed with them all her life, did the housework, cooked, baked, washed, fought against creditors, was a second mother for Jenny's children and a second wife for Karl. It was therefore only right and proper that she remained with Jenny and Karl even after her death. She was buried in the cemetery of Highgate alongside the couple she had served all her life.

Little is known about Lenchen's origins. It seems that she was born in 1820 – and not in 1823, as it says on the tombstone – in a village in the vicinity of St Wendel in the Palatinate. Her father, who came from a family of peasants, was a baker and had seven children. Lenchen was eight or nine years old when she was sent to a rich family in Trier as a nursemaid. She had to take care of a baby and do an amount of housework that Baroness von Westphalen thought too hard. She took pity on Lenchen and brought her into her own home, as a replacement for her late daughter Laura.

When she came to Brussels, Lenchen was 25 years old, six years younger than Jenny, blonde and slim, and so similar to Jenny in her appearance that in pictures she has often been mistaken for her mistress. She had bright blue eyes, a high forehead and a strong chin. She was obviously a woman who knew what she wanted and was not afraid to say so. She had many suitors and could have made a good match more than once, but she stayed with Jenny and Karl, even when shop-keepers' credit and her wages were not forthcoming.

Helene Demuth's position in the Marx family was only endangered once, when in 1851 she became pregnant and refused to give the name of the father of her child. Stephan Born, a young German typesetter, who knew the family Marx well in Brussels, writes that he received a letter from Jenny 'with the sad news, but with indignation between the lines, that her faithful and untirin, maid who was a quasi member of the family had left her'.[2] But this is not what happened. Lenchen did not leave, she remained; and in June 1851 she gave birth to a boy, who was christened Frederick Demuth, adopted by an English couple of the working class and played no further role in the life of the Marx family. The relationship between Jenny and Lenchen was not affected by this event, at least not outwardly, but in her autobiographical essay 'A Short Outline of a Turbulent Life' she writes: 'There occurred an event in the early summer of 1851 which I shall not touch on in detail, but which contributed greatly to the increase of our outer and inner worries'.[3] But more later about this.

In April 1845, almost at the same time that Lenchen came to Brussels, Jenny made the acquaintance of the man about whom Karl had told her so much, Friedrich Engels, the son of the textile manufacturer from Barmen. He had left his father's office, because business life disgusted him – he called it huck-stering. He wanted to live as a freelance author and advocate of a new world order. He believed in the future of communism. He had written to Marx: 'If one does not write, it is possible to be a bourgeois and a huckster at the same time, but it is not possible actively to carry on communist propaganda and at the same time huckstering and business. I am leaving here at Easter.'⁴

Engels was 25 years old, only two years younger than Marx, but his whole appearance, reminiscent of a Prussian officer, was so youthful that he did not look his age. He talked volubly, liked to laugh and enjoyed the venial pleasures of wine, women and song. He often talked about England, which he seemed to know very well, and expressed the opinion that in the near future the British workers would overthrow the ruling bourgeoisie by revolutionary action.

Jenny was present during many of their conversations and got the impression that her husband knew very much more about the historic evolution of capitalism to communism than the son of the Barmen capitalist who advocated communism so passionately. However, she soon realized that Engels had much closer contacts with the workers than Karl. She was therefore not surprised when Karl told her that Engels had proposed they should spend a few weeks in England and meet up with the leaders of English trades unions, with Chartists and with German artisan communists. Jenny had no objections, but she insisted that the problem of the financing of the trip should be solved first. As soon as it was solved, she would go with Jennychen and Lenchen to Trier and spend the summer there with her mother. Meanwhile she spent many stimulating evenings with Engels and Karl in cafés in the centre of Brussels, where they met friends from Paris, as well as Russians, Poles and Germans in political exile; among them was the famous young poet Ferdinand Freiligrath, who had as many passionate admirers among the German youth as Herwegh and, like the latter, was persecuted by the Prussian authorities as a dangerous demagogue.

Marx had criticized Freiligrath bitterly in the *Rheinische Zeitung* and deplored the fact that he had accepted a pension from King Frederick William IV. At that time Freiligrath had believed in 'pure art' – '*l'art pour l'art*' – for 'the poet stands on a higher plane than the party's battlements'.⁵ Four years later, however, the revolutionary fever of the German youth drove the poet from his ivory tower into the political maelstrom. He wrote a small volume of poems entitled *Professions of Faith* with the subtitle 'Contemporary History' and the resolution expressed in the preface 'to stand firmly and imperturbably on the side of those who oppose the reactionaries with head and with heart.'[6] Freiligrath had these poems printed, although the censor had prohibited them, had given up his royal pension and gone into exile in Brussels. Marx was so impressed that he visited the poet immediately after his arrival in Brussels, for 'he wanted to make amends for the wrong that the *Rheinische Zeitung* had done Freiligrath before he stood on the battlements of the party'.[7] Freiligrath received his former critic 'the interesting, pleasant, unassuming chap Karl Marx',[8] in a friendly manner and joined the small band of young people gathered around Marx and Engels.

Jenny's brother Edgar was among them. Jenny had mixed feelings when he appeared in Brussels. She had been happy to hear that he had passed his state exam, despite years of neglected studies, and had obtained a position at the regional court in Trier; she was also happy about Edgar's engagement to Lina Schöler. She hoped that Edgar would make a good career in Trier and ease her mother's old age by his presence. But Edgar was a restless spirit: why should he work himself to death for an administration which sooner or later would cease to exist because it was opposed to the world order propagated by his brother-in-law? Better to belong to the leaders of the revolution than to its victims.

When Marx and Engels finally started at the beginning of July on their research trip to London and Manchester, Jenny stayed two further weeks in Brussels. Apart from Lenchen and her brother, a young Prussian officer Joseph Weydemeyer, lived with her. He had left military service because he was a convinced communist and had come to Brussels like other revolutionary young Germans, because he wanted to study the new gospel at its source. Jenny found him very congenial and he remained her friend – just as his future wife Louise would – throughout her life.

Jenny enjoyed the six weeks she spent with her mother in Trier thoroughly. She wrote to Karl: 'I have never felt any better than now in dear old Germany;[9] you must agree it takes courage to say this to you arch-German-haters. But I have it, this courage, and in spite of all, in spite of all, life is good in this old land of sins. At any rate I have only encountered the pettiest and meanest conditions in magnificent France and Belgium. People here are little, very little, all of life here is a miniature edition; however, the heroes over there are no giants either and for the average person life there is not one whit better. It may be different for men, but for the woman who is meant for bearing children, for sewing, cooking, mending I sing the praises of our miserable Germany'.[10]

Jenny's mother noted with satisfaction the visible physical and mental improvement of her daughter in the course of her stay in Trier. She hoped that Jenny and Karl would give up their nomadic life and return to Germany. She worried about the future of both her children. It was unfortunate that Jenny and Edgar had fallen into the political quicksand of the time because of Karl's communist convictions. She was entirely in favour of helping the poor, but she was alarmed when Jenny talked of the bloody revolution that Karl prophesied. Her late husband had told her of the terrible things that happened during the French Revolution and that the poor in France had been just as poor after the Revolution as before. Would it not be the same in Germany? There was, not without reason, the saying: '*La révolution dévore ses enfants.*'

Jenny thought differently, or pretended she thought differently, and she could not do otherwise without betraying her husband. Karl believed firmly in the revolution and considered it his duty to make preparations for it. As Karl's wife, the mother of his daughter and now heavily pregnant with his second child, Jenny had no other choice than to return to the 'pauper colony' of their Brussels exile. She wrote to Karl that she would take care of the 'great affair' upstairs in their little house and afterwards move down again. He could sleep in his present study and work undisturbed, while she was with the children. In quiet moments she would come and help clean up his room. Edgar's presence worried her. The house was not large enough for all of them and Lenchen. Her mother thought it would be best to rent a room for Edgar somewhere else, perhaps in the Hotel Bois Sauvage.

She had heard from Weydemeyer that the political zealot Moses Hess was thinking of getting married: she wondered what girl he had become involved with. And Engels, about whose affairs with women she had heard so much, 'had he come back solo or *à deux*?'[11] Karl had told her before their departure, that Engels had taken up with a young Irish textile-worker while he was in Manchester working in his father's firm. She had shown him the workers' hovels that he had described so movingly in his book. Jenny often thought about this young Irish girl and wondered why an intelligent man like Engels would get involved with a working-class woman. It embarrassed her when she heard that Engels had brought the young girl to Brussels and was living with her without being married.

Stephan Born reports that Karl and Jenny were present at a social gathering of the Brussels branch of the German Workers' Union. 'Engels with his – lady' were there. 'A fair distance separated both couples. When I approached Marx in order to greet him and his wife he gave me to understand by a glance and a meaningful smile that his wife strictly refused to make the acquaintance of that – lady. Concerning questions of honour and morals the noble lady was intransigent. She would have been outraged if anybody had ever asked her to make a compromise in such matters. This intermezzo increased my high regard for Mrs Marx. By bringing his mistress to this group of mostly working-class people Engels risked the reproach often made that the rich sons of manufacturers used the young girls of the people for their pleasure.'[12]

Jenny had good reason to be grateful to Engels for the financial and political support he gave her husband and her family for decades; she often corresponded with him, shared her everyday worries with him and kept him informed about her husband's illnesses but she always addressed him as 'Dear Mr Engels'. She never used either his first name Friedrich or Fritz, nor the nickname 'General' that was later customarily used by members of her family.

'The great catastrophe', as Jenny called her confinement, because it coincided with the completion of Karl's book *The German Ideology*, occurred on 26 September 1845. It was again a girl and they called her Laura in memory of Jenny's sister Laura who had died in childhood. As the mother of two babies and the wife of a man who needed her to copy his illegible letters and manuscripts, Jenny did not have much time to take care of the household – Lenchen was in charge of that and she was much better at it than Jenny. As far as merchants and shopkeepers were concerned Lenchen was the mistress of the household, Jenny the *grande dame* to whom you took off your hat. Wilhelm Liebknecht, a close friend of the Marxes, says: 'Lenchen was the dictator in the house of Marx, Jenny the ruler.'[13]

Thanks to this division of labour Jenny could devote herself to her husband's business and ideas. She took part in the conversations between Karl and Engels about *The German Ideology*, a book which aimed to supersede once and for all the superficiality of such German philosophers as Feuerbach and other prophets of the so-called 'true socialism'; and to clear the way for their own ideas of 'scientific socialism' and the inevitable outbreaks of revolutions which would finally bring about a communist world order; for 'we do not consider communism a condition that has to be established, an ideal towards which reality has to reach. We call communism the *real* movement which will cancel the present condition.'[14]

Jenny was impressed by such words. Compared with the eternal uncertainty of the bourgeois world, the cut-throat competition, the money-grubbing on the one hand, the hunger and misery on the other, communist society seemed to embody the ideal of genuine humanity. In order to realize this ideal it was necessary to prepare the workers of the world for the conquest of political power. This was done through the

communist correspondence committees which Karl and
Engels set up after their return from England, with Jenny
acting as their Brussels secretary.

In the middle of March 1846 Jenny's mother became
seriously ill and Jenny again had to return to Trier. During her
absence Lenchen took care of the household and Karl wrote
her that there had been a complete break between him and
Wilhelm Weitling, the most prominent representative of
utopian communism. Karl said he had read the riot act to this
windbag of a journeyman tailor. When she heard this, Jenny
answered: 'There must have been a terrible row with you. I am
glad I was not there when it happened.'[15] And yet she was
happy 'that you, my dear Karl, always keep your head and
remain master of your impatience and longing. How much I
love you because of your courage. You are my man!'[16] She
reminded him that his book should appear soon, because 'the
false prophets have polluted the field',[17] but also because she
knew that without royalties from literary publications their
family could not exist.

Marx did not need such an admonition from his wife. What
he needed was a publisher for the voluminous manuscript *The
German Ideology*. But he did not find one. In spite of all their
efforts the work remained unpublished and became, as Engels
wrote later, 'prey to the gnawing criticism of mice'.[18] The last
summer months in Brussels were particularly difficult for
Marx and his family. He wrote to his friend Weydemeyer:
'You know that I am in great financial straits. I have been
forced to pawn our last pieces of gold and silver and a great
deal of our linen merely in order to survive. I have even given
up our own home to economize and have moved back to the
Bois Sauvage. I would have had to employ another nursemaid, since the baby is now being weaned.'[19]

Jenny became sick and stayed in bed, as she always did when
the domestic pressures got too intense. She was pregnant for
the third time and was expecting a child at the end of the year.
Lenchen had to take care of the entire household, for 'my wife
cannot do much, because she is ill and has to stay in bed most

of the time'.[20] Thus Marx to Hess. He himself made hectic
preparations for all kinds of projects to earn money. He turned
to friends and acquaintances with the proposal that they
should buy shares in a literary review he was planning to
publish with the aim of propagating the principles of political
economy. The price per share was 25 thalers. He also drew
promissory notes on members of communist correspondence
committees whom, he thought, owed him money. And he
continued to urge his mother to pay him his share of his
father's estate.

However, while Marx and his family faced formidable
problems of sheer survival, it was also a time of intensive work
on the establishment of an international workers' movement
on the basis of scientific communism. Assisted by Engels he
made the communist correspondence committee in Brussels
the centre of the communist world-view, the 'Marx Party' as
it was called – a party that supported anyone and anything that
promised help 'without having any stupid moral scruples'.[21]

Jenny's brother was for a time a member of the Marx Party
and signed some resolutions which his brother-in-law issued
against such diluters of his gospel as the editor of the New
York *Volks Tribüne*, Hermann Kriege. This charlatan, who
was considered to be the literary representative of German
communism in America, was compromising Europe's communists by transforming atheistic communism into a religious
love-feast. Marx attacked him just as bitterly as he had
attacked the sentimental communistic world-reformer
Weitling two months before. The fools wanted to found a
political movement upon feelings, instead of analysing the
economic laws of bourgeois society. Feeling is not everything
– scientific knowledge is!

The authoritarian attitude of his brother-in-law began to
irritate Edgar. He was by nature a kind, somewhat lazy,
person who hoped to get a good job as a result of Karl's
revolution. Since for the time being nothing seemed to be
happening and since the collapse of his efforts to get a good
position, where he would not have to work too hard, he had

decided to go to America, along with so many other young Germans of the time. Even his brother-in-law, Karl, had toyed with the idea of going to America during his first months in Brussels. But only for a short time, for he was convinced that the social conditions for a communist movement were more favourable in the old world than in the new. Such considerations did not interest Jenny's brother. As long as he was in Brussels without a position, he relied for financial support on his mother, much to Marx's annoyance. Marx, who worked hard but earned nothing, was angry at the way that 'the sluggard Edgar' squandered his wife's fortune. But he agreed that his third child, a son, born in December 1846, be given the name Edgar – an event which satisfied his profound feeling that the making of history belonged to the male sex.

Christmas of 1846 was the last in Europe for Jenny's brother. In the spring of 1847 he left for Texas, encouraged by his well-to-do German relatives who gave him the necessary financial support. It was hard for Jenny to say goodbye to her brother. She tried to comfort Lina Schöler, Edgar's disconsolate fiancée, by writing to her that Edgar would surely return to Germany, when the new order of society made it possible for him to do so, 'for we are certainly approaching the period of dissolution, transformation and the time is perhaps not far when people of Edgar's talent, his personal courage, his chivalrous thinking are needed. He will then surely come back home and will stand at your and mother's side as adviser, protector and supporter.'[22]

The years around 1850 were indeed years of political dissolution, but for Jenny they were also years of great expectations. As her husband's confidante and co-operator she was convinced that the transformations of European society that he predicted would soon occur. The Marx Party would then come to power and all the privations of their present life would be over.

In fact, the financial condition of the family had improved somewhat after Edgar's birth. Karl had received some money from his Dutch uncle and Jenny from her mother. In the middle of January 1847 they moved into a small house in the rue d'Orléans, Faubourg de Namour, which became a meeting-place for the disaffected, attracting exiles from Germany, like Wilhelm Wolff, always called 'Lupus' by the Marxes. He was a journalist and teacher, who had escaped from jail following a conviction for offences against the Prussian press laws. As the son of Silesian serfs his childhood had been bitter, and he had realized early that he could only escape the fate of his parents by rigorous self-discipline. With the aid of his parish priest he entered high school and later university. He studied philology and became the leader of the Breslau students union and an advocate of revolutionary principles.

Another member of the group was the watchmaker Josef Moll, known as 'Jupp'. He had been expelled from Cologne, was now a member of the League of the Just in London, and had come to Brussels to recruit Marx and Engels to the League. The League had about 250 members, mostly German artisans, who met three times a week for lectures or political and cultural discussion. The aim of the League was to educate the young in the ideal of a society without exploitation, oppression or undeserved poverty. It espoused communism, but not the scientific communism that Marx and Engels propagated. For Moll and his London comrades the declarations of the Brussels communists had at first been suspect. 'We thought your idea was to establish a kind of aristocracy of scholars and to rule the people from above your new seat of the gods.'[23] However, they had finally decided to debate with Marx and Engels a joint programme for all the communist committees.

In the discussions with Moll, in which Jenny participated while Engels was in Paris, Marx declared at first that he was opposed to all conspiratorial societies and that he considered communist plots hatched in secret societies as childish nonsense. Communism, as he understood it, was the seizure of power by the proletariat according to strict economic laws. The workers have to be told that it is their historic role to break the power of the bourgeoisie by revolutionary action; they should not be confused by sentimental talk about Christian charity, but reminded that communism was not hatched in the brains of a few student conspirators, but the inevitable future form of society.

Jenny soon felt that Karl's explanations, made in his usual authoritarian manner, did not please the good watchmaker Moll. She remembered a letter in which the communist artisans of London complained about the arrogance of the intellectuals, who 'whenever they get together with workers, set off their learned bombs and wrap themselves up in a supernatural halo, who do not know how to gain the friend-ship of the workers, which they repel instead of attract – and you, you *proletarians* of Brussels have this accursed scholarly arrogance to a particularly high degree'.[24] She advised Karl to prove to these artisan communists of London that he valued their political efforts by joining their League. Marx did so, but insisted that the name be changed from the League of the Just to the Communist League. Engels, who was trying to gain converts for the communist cause among the German workers in Paris, proposed that Marx should think about the text of a communist confession of faith. He, like Jenny, was of the opinion that too many false prophets had polluted the field.

Jenny was unhappy about the bitter polemic attack which Karl started in the *Deutsche Brüsseler Zeitung* against a former colleague on the *Rheinische Zeitung* Karl Peter Heinzen, partly because it was he who had been so friendly to her when she arrived in Brussels. But Heinzen had provoked Karl's anger by an article in which he declared that if communism insisted on the abolition of all private property, it would destroy individual enterprise and freedom. Jenny agreed that it was unfortunate that Heinzen had expressed such an opinion, but she knew that at heart he was a revolutionary and a fighter for a just society. It was a pity that the common cause was weak-ened by such controversies carried out in public, just now when unrest was seething everywhere. Riots had broken out in Paris and Berlin because of the high price of bread; workers had stormed bakeries. There was discontent among the workers in Brussels too and the Marx family itself experienced the scarcity of bread. There was often no money even to post the letters to the various communist correspondence committees.

This was the financial situation in which Marx found himself when he was invited by the Communist League to come to London in November 1847 as a member of an international meeting to commemorate the Polish revolution of 1830. He wrote to the well-to-do Russian journalist Paul Annenkow 'when I undertook the journey I had to leave my family in the most desolate and difficult situation. Not only because my wife and my children are sick, but because my economic condition is so critical at the moment and my poor wife is constantly being harassed by creditors because of our miserable financial predicament'.[25] Since Marx knew that like most men Annenkow venerated Jenny, he added: 'In this situation you would truly save me from the worst, if you could send my wife a sum of 100 or 200 francs'.[26] He added his wife must not know that he had made such a request.

After Marx had temporarily suppressed his domestic worries, he plunged into work. He declared in his speech that the signal for the liberation of Poland from the Russian yoke would come from England. For 'of all countries it is England where the contrast between proletariat and bourgeoisie is most developed. The victory of British workers over the British bourgeoisie is therefore decisive for the victory of all oppressed over their oppressors. Hence, Poland cannot be liberated in Poland but in England.'[27]

These words were greeted with great applause and the Communist League of London requested officially that Marx draw up a document of the basic principles of the Communist Party and present it before the end of the year to his German party members in London.

Marx returned to Brussels in the middle of December and pretended to be surprised when Jenny told him that she had received 200 francs from her Russian admirer Annenkow. For the time being she need not worry what to give the children for Christmas or how to pay the food bills. The last weeks of 1847 were hard work for Marx. A world trade crisis and the price rises it precipitated led to noisy protests everywhere in Europe and the time was obviously ripe for revolution. It was therefore important, particularly at Christmas when Christianity was uppermost in people's minds, to show the workers of the world a communist confession of faith. Engels, still in Paris, proposed that it be called 'The Communist Manifesto'. During Christmas and the first weeks of the new year Marx worked with Jenny as his secretary on the text of a proclamation as influential as any in the annals of history.

Preparations for a family Christmas party, which Jenny had to discuss with Lenchen and about which she corresponded with her mother in Trier, interrupted her work on the Manifesto. There was, in addition, the Christmas party of the German Workers' Union, at which Jenny had to help decorating the hall. Karl, the main speaker, made a toast to Belgium's democracy, contrasting it to the absolutism of the other European states and calling it a model for all Europe because it guaranteed free speech and assembly.

The *Deutsche Brüsseler Zeitung* published a long report about the New Year's celebrations of the German Workers' Union: 'The banquet on New Year's Eve was another step toward fraternization and strengthening of democracy in several countries. No discordant note disturbed this respectable and enjoyable party. A number of ladies in full evening dress took part and we observed beautiful women applauding vigorously. The banquet was followed by music and then by a dramatic performance, where Madame Dr Marx showed a brilliant talent for recitation. It is very impressive to watch exceptionally gifted ladies trying to improve the intellectual faculties of the proletariat'.[28]

This New Year's Eve was a high point in Jenny's life. She was dancing with her beloved husband into the fateful year of 1848, cheerful and confident, for the future lay full of promise before her. Under Karl's direction she copied the last pages of *The Communist Manifesto* which was emphatically requested

by the Communist League of London: Marx sent it off at the
end of January.

He could not have realized that he was sending into the
world a work that would compete with the Bible in its effect
and circulation. It was much more important to him to receive
on 9 February from his mother in Trier an advance of 6,000
francs from his paternal inheritance, negotiated by his Dutch
uncle Lion Philips. Now he was rid of the eternal daily
financial worries and could devote himself completely to the
coming revolutionary struggles. For, as Jenny writes in her
autobiographical essay: 'On the Belgian horizon too it was
becoming dark. There was fear of the workers, the social
element of the masses. The police, the army, the militia,
everybody was called up to serve; all were ready for battle.
The German workers also thought that the time had come to
look for weapons. Daggers, revolvers etc. were bought. Karl
provided the means gladly, for he had just received some
money.'[29]

On 26 February the news reached Brussels that a revolution
had broken out in Paris, that the King had fled and that France
was again a republic. The call of the Gallic Cock was the long-
awaited sign. 'Our time', cried Jenny, 'the time of democracy
is coming',[30] and Karl added 'the flames of the Tuileries and of
the Royal Palace are the sunrise of the proletariat'.[31] Riots also
occurred in Brussels. Large crowds gathered in the squares at
the centre of the city, in cafés and taverns, listening attentively
as youthful orators demanded '*liberté*' and '*egalité*' and '*la
République*'. The guardians of law and order were horrified
and considered how to protect Belgium from the flames of the
French Revolution. As a first step they decided to expel all
foreign revolutionary agitators, and by 27 February had
already begun to prepare lists of known German communists.

Marx knew nothing of it and had other plans. On the day
when he heard that a revolution had broken out in Paris, he
had moved with his family into the Hotel Bois Sauvage and
had suggested that Jenny go to her mother in Trier with
Lenchen and the children, so that he could carry out his work

unhindered by domestic responsibilities. While Jenny was making preparations for her return to Trier, Marx went to London, where he held discussions with the leaders of the Communist League about the current political situation, and proposed to transfer the main office of the Communist League from London to Paris. He addressed a letter to the provisional French government with a request for the cancellation of the expulsion order issued against him by King Louis Philippe. On his return to Brussels he found a letter signed by the new government minister Ferdinand Flocon with the words: '*la tyrannie vous a banni – la France libre vous rouvre ses portes*'.[32] 'Tyranny banished you – a free France reopens its doors to you!'

However, the events of the next few days took a precipitous turn and prevented Marx from leaving Belgium peacefully. On the night of 4 March, police officers entered his room in the Hotel Bois Sauvage and arrested him. He was accused of having given money to German workers in Brussels for the purchase of weapons. Jenny writes: 'They dragged him away in the night, I run after them terribly afraid and try to find influential people to discover what they were up to. In the darkness of night I run from house to house. Suddenly a guard grabs hold of me, arrests me and throws me into a dark jail. It was the place where they put up homeless beggars, rootless wanderers, unfortunate, lost women. I am pushed into a dark cell. I sob as I enter, and one of my unfortunate fellow sufferers offers me her bed. It was a hard wooden bunk. I fall down on it'.[33]

When daylight came, Jenny discovered that Karl was being escorted by a military police force and expelled from Belgium upon order of King Leopold. She herself had to undergo a two hour cross-examination, during which 'they did not get much out of me'.[34] She certainly did not reveal, what she later admitted in the review of her life, that Karl *had* given money to the German workers to buy arms. Jenny's discretion was absolute.

After her examination was abandoned without result, the

police took her to a coach and 'I arrived back home to my poor little babies only in the evening'.[35] Then with Lenchen's help she began packing her personal effects, sold what could be sold, but left her silver and better linen in the care of the bookseller Vogler. Accompanied by the young printer Stephan Born she travelled back to the Paris which she had left three years ago. 'It was a very cold, cloudy day, the last in the month of February [it was actually the beginning of March] and we found it very difficult to keep the babies warm, the youngest being barely a year old.'[36]

When she reached Paris, she parted from her young companion, who reported the strain caused by the events of the last few days: 'A deep sadness lay on her pure features. We shook hands and said goodbye when she had reached her provisional home. Everything had been provisional for her, a real home for herself and her children she had never known'.[37]

7

The Year of Decision 1848–1849

I

Jenny, her children and Lenchen found lodgings in a small Parisian hotel called the Manchester and she was very happy when Karl appeared a day later. They were both impressed by the signs of fighting in Paris. They saw barricades half torn down next to mountains of paving stones, overturned coaches, smashed window-panes and everywhere masses of people waving the *tricolore* and singing the Marseillaise. The King was gone – long live the Republic!

Marx knew that now he had to act decisively and show both friend and foe his true stature. But first he had to settle accounts with the Belgian authorities, who had dared to arrest a German democrat and thrust his wife – 'a Prussian aristocrat, whose sole crime was that she shares the democratic opinions of her husband'[1] – into jail where she had to spend a whole night in a cell with thieves and prostitutes. Thus, in a letter to the Parisian newspaper *Reforme*, Marx denounced the humiliations he and Jenny had suffered in Brussels, and Engels wrote a fierce article about it in the *Northern Star*.

In Brussels, liberal deputies brought the *'affaire Marx'* to the attention of the City Council, and the Minister of Justice was instructed to carry out an investigation of the circumstances that had led to the arrests. Since all their efforts failed to prove that Marx had furnished arms to the workers, they dismissed the Assistant Deputy of Police Daxbeek. This ended the matter as far as the Belgian Minister of Justice was concerned. Whether or not Dr Marx had given money for the purchase of arms, he was an agitator and had to leave Belgium, since he had blatantly violated the promise he gave at his arrival to abstain from all political publications.

In March 1848 Paris was a witch's kitchen of rising expectations. News about street fighting and battles on barricades poured in from all over Europe. In Vienna the long-suppressed anger of the people had driven the reactionary Metternich from power; in Berlin the King had to submit to the will of the people and honour the revolutionaries his troops had killed, by attending their funeral; there was unrest as far as Warsaw and St Petersburg. For thousands of German artisans in Paris who dreamt of a united, democratic Germany and even more for writers and intellectuals who had been expelled because of their convictions, the hope of returning home and helping in a reordering of society grew from day to day. However, there were basic differences of opinion over the way to arrive at this goal, which turned old friends into bitter enemies. Two sets of such casualties were Marx and Herwegh, and Jenny and Herwegh's wife Emma.

When Marx arrived in Paris he found Herwegh in a state of euphoric revolutionary enthusiasm. In passionate tones the poet told Marx that the Germans in Paris were beginning to rally and arm themselves, and that he and his friends planned to dispatch to Germany a force of four or five thousand well-trained volunteers, who would establish a republic by force of arms. Marx was surprised and asked who the leader of this legion was. Herwegh declared that he, Herr von Bornstedt and some other German democrats in Paris, had established a union called the German Democratic Society, of which he was president. He hoped that Marx would join this society. But Marx was not about to accept a secondary role in the coming German revolution. Together with Engels, who had also come to Paris, and the London-based communists Schapper, Bauer and Moll, he founded the German Workers' Union. When Jenny tried to talk with Emma Herwegh about the situation, she was told that her husband had only founded the German Workers' Union because he was envious of Herwegh who would play a prominent role in the coming German republic. Jenny contradicted her vigorously. She explained that Karl considered an invasion of Germany by a group of amateur soldiers not only senseless, but potentially dangerous inasmuch as revolutionary feelings in Germany could easily become nationalistic. An invasion of Germany from France, even if it was led by German workers, was still an invasion and could hardly lead to the establishment of a republic. Emma's response was to throw Jenny out of her house, with the parting words that Karl would never become the President of a democratic Germany if he was too cowardly to fight for it. But fight both Jenny and Karl did, if not on the barricades. Marx's weapon was his pen and the power of the word. He fought his battles in endless newspaper articles, appeals, speeches, meetings and letters. In March 1848 he composed jointly with Engels a pamphlet entitled 'Demands of the Communist Party in Germany'. It was printed in Paris under the heading: 'Workers of the World Unite' and contained seventeen demands. Many of them, such as the first – 'Germany will become a united indivisible Republic' – were shared by many Germans who were not communists. Another, the thirteenth – 'Complete separation of Church and State' – was suggested by the American Constitution. The final demand – to establish national workshops to guarantee the workers' right to work – had also been proclaimed by the new revolutionary French government.

For Jenny, a keen participant in her husband's political

activities, these were hectic weeks. In a letter to Joseph Weydemeyer, an old friend of the Marx Party and editor of the *Westphälische Dampfboot* in Hamm, she wrote:

> My husband is again so busy with work and running about in this great city that he asks me to request that you publish in the *Westphälische Dampfboot* the fact that several societies have been organized here. However, the 'German Workers' Union', led by the London Germans Schapper, Bauer and Moll and the Germans from Brussels Marx, Wolff, Engels, Wallau and Born (who are also in direct contact with the Chartists in England through Harney and Jones) have nothing in common with the 'German Democratic Association' presided over by Börnstein, Bornstedt, Herwegh, Volk, Decker etc., a group that hoists the black–red–gold flag (the Bundestag has just stolen a march on them in this matter), talks of Father Blücher and is being drilled by discharged Prussian officers. It is absolutely essential to dissociate ourselves clearly from this group, because it will make a fool of the Germans. Should this information come too late for the *Dampfboot*, please write an article about it for the German newspapers you have access to in the south. Try to get this information in as many German newspapers as possible.[2]

Jenny concluded this appeal in support of her husband's cause with the words: 'I would like to tell you much more about the interesting goings-on here that are getting more turbulent by the minute (400,000 workers will march to the Hotel de Ville this evening), the mobs are getting bigger again, however I am so overworked with house, family and my three little ones that I have time only to send you and your dear wife cordial regards from afar. *Salut et Fraternité.*' She signed herself '*Citoyenne and Vagabonde* Jenny Marx'.[3]

Jenny would have been much busier with house, family and little ones if she had not had Lenchen's help, a fact which she considered so much a matter of course that she hardly mentions it in her letters. But while Lenchen took care of house and family, she was able to accompany Karl to his heated debates with Engels and other comrades in Parisian cafés. Scornfully they watched the departure of Herwegh's volunteers to Germany at the beginning of April, 'for we have nothing in common with the great crusade starting here to conquer the German Republic'[4] and decided to conquer Germany not with weapons but with the fiery words of a great newspaper. This decision was much more compatible with Marx's journalistic instincts than the war cries of many of his fellow communists. Above all else it was important to him to make 'his' movement into a mass movement by means of effective propaganda. Only after it had become that, only when the workers confessed to being communists, was the time ripe for a revolutionary seizure of power and the establishment of the dictatorship of the proletariat. These considerations were a further proof for Jenny that the man she loved would not plunge carelessly into revolutionary adventures, but was steadily pursuing his goal of a better order of society. 'To remain steady and reasonable in the midst of confusion . . . that I applaud. You are my man.'[5]

II

After the decision to found a newspaper had been reached, questions of money and place of publication had to be resolved. Marx, the anti-Prussian Rhinelander, shook his head when Berlin was mentioned. To be sure he had pleasant memories of his student years in Berlin, but the Prussian capital was an unsuitable place for a political daily newspaper, even though the revolution was now picking up there too. Marx wanted to go back to Cologne, where he had started his journalistic career and where the name of the newspaper, suppressed in 1843 by Prussian censorship, was still remembered: the former *Rheinische Zeitung* would rise again as the *Neue Rheinische Zeitung*. The problem of getting financial support might also be solved, for it was hoped that some of the liberal industrialists who had supported the *Rheinische Zeitung* would become shareholders of the new paper. In any case, the

attempt had to be made and it was therefore necessary to go to
Cologne as soon as possible. Marx and Engels left Paris on 6
April. Jenny, Lenchen and the children returned to Trier.

Soon after his arrival in Cologne, Karl applied to a police
commission with the request for the freedom of the city of
Cologne. He explained that he had lived in Cologne in the
years 1842–3 as editor of the former *Rheinische Zeitung*; after
the paper stopped publication he had lived abroad and had
given up his Prussian citizenship. But, as a result of recent
events, he had decided to settle in Cologne with his family. As
his address he mentioned Apostelstrasse 7. *Nomen est omen*: it
was the right address for the apostle of a new order of society.
While he and Engels were considering how best to approach
Rhenish industrialists *vis-à-vis* the *Neue Rheinische Zeitung*,
they heard that Moses Hess, a co-founder of the old *Rheinische
Zeitung*, together with Anneke and Gottschalk, members of
the Communist League of Cologne, had already issued an
appeal to found a new *Rheinische Zeitung*, which they hoped to
finance by the sale of subscriptions. The scatterbrain Hess 'had
once again proved a smart operator'.[6] It was necessary to act
quickly in order to get ahead of him. Reliable emissaries were
dispatched to establish direct contact with former shareholders, asking them to support an organ for democracy in
Germany. The word communism must not be mentioned.
'Communism is the major shock-word. A confessed communist would be stoned.'[7] But it should be possible to obtain
support in the Rhineland for a paper under a democratic flag.
Marx hoped for a sum of 30,000 thalers, made up of 600 shares
at 50 thalers each. He soon discovered, however, that this was
not easy. Most of the former shareholders refused to offer
their support. Engels even failed to get money from his father
in Barmen. 'It's damned useless to hope for shares here . . .
People fear discussions of social questions like the pest; they
call it stirring up incitement . . . The fact is that at bottom
even these radical bourgeois look upon us as their future
enemies and they don't want to give us any weapons that we
might direct against them. My old man categorically refused

to give anything. He considers even the *Kölner Zeitung* a paragon of incitement and instead of 1,000 thalers he would rather send us 1,000 grapeshot.'[8]

Jenny watched events in Cologne closely. Her position in Trier, as the wife of a well-known leader of the revolutionary movement that kept the world in suspense, was interesting and exciting. People she hardly knew asked her what they should do in such turbulent times. Should they vote for democrats or republicans? What would happen to the King? Wouldn't everybody defend his own property? Jenny replied in the spirit of her husband that they were at a great historic turning-point, and that the coming order of society would be determined by the will of the workers and not by the purses of the capitalists. What was happening in Paris now was but the prelude to a worldwide development.

Caroline von Westphalen shook her head, when she heard her daughter talk like this. The workers she knew were incapable of founding a new social order, their perspectives being limited to earning enough money to feed, clothe, and house their families. It was pure illusion to believe that workers were able to administer the affairs of a city, let alone a state. Jenny should know that her father had done much more for the working people in Trier than he could have done had he himself been a worker. Jenny agreed, but said that it was necessary to educate the workers for the role they had to fulfil in the future by meetings, discussions, evening courses and above all by progressive newspaper articles.

That was the function of the *Neue Rheinische Zeitung*. Its first number appeared, much to Jenny's joy, on 1 June 1848, a month earlier than planned. She had been almost three months with her mother in Trier and had seen Karl only occasionally. But now she moved to Cologne, to take up the fight for the future at his side. She found a little apartment for the family in Cäcilienstrasse, quite close to Karl's office. Thus she entered the centre of the political storm which the *Neue Rheinische Zeitung* tried to intensify by its commentaries. Engels told her that the political programme of the paper comprised two

major goals: establishment of a united, indivisible, democratic
German republic, and war with Russia and the restoration of
Poland.

The bloody suppression of the Parisian workers at the
beginning of June upset the hopes that had been raised by the
February Revolution in many parts of Europe. The columns
of the *Neue Rheinische Zeitung* now emphasized the dangers of
counter-revolution and it became doubly important to keep
close contact with the workers' unions that existed in many
German towns. This meant such an incredible amount of
work for Marx that he had hardly any time for his family and
he needed Jenny's help to meet all his demands. She copied his
articles, answered his letters, conferred with the rest of the
paper's staff – Engels, Wolff, Dronke and Weerth – when Karl
was not in Cologne, and was responsible for taking care of the
family. She was dismayed, when she learned that Geiger,
the Commissioner of Police in Cologne, had rejected Karl's
request for the recovery of his Prussian citizenship and that he
and his family would have to remain foreigners. The possi-
bility of being pushed back into exile made Jenny shudder,
after what she had experienced in Paris and in Brussels during
the five years of her marriage. She was speechless when she
heard that Engels 'was longing to get back to the sleepless
nights of exile away from this boring philistine farce called
German revolution'.[9] The future for Karl, for her and their
family, depended on the success of the *Neue Rheinische Zeitung*
and on the politics it stood for. It already had 5,000 readers and
was a voice that could not be ignored.

On his initiative the first Rhenish Democratic Congress
took place in Cologne in the middle of August with representatives from seventeen workers' unions of various towns in
the Rhineland. A resolution was passed to found workers'
unions in all German towns and to send an appeal to the
National Assembly in Frankfurt demanding a German social
democracy, a 'Red Republic', instead of the black–red–gold
one proposed by the bourgeois politicians. In the Prussian
capital, where counter-revolutionary forces began stirring,

just as in Paris, notice was being taken of the activities of the editor-in-chief of the *Neue Rheinische Zeitung* and of his 'provocative articles'. Thought was given to expelling Marx as an undesirable alien. It was also hoped that supporters of the newspaper, intimidated by its radical tone, would refuse to give further money for it. This, in fact, was what came to pass. The financial condition of the paper was already so precarious in August, that Marx had to pay the printer out of his own pocket. Since he had no means to finance the paper by himself, he decided to undertake a tour through Germany to contact possible financial backers in Berlin and Vienna, and to discuss the next phase of the German revolution in meetings with workers.

During his absence Engels acted as editor-in-chief of the paper and Jenny, helped by Lenchen, was fully responsible for the family. She used the time of Karl's absence to make their little Cologne apartment more homely by unpacking the silver, linen and china that Vogler had sent her from Brussels. Her best friend at this time was Lina Schöler, the abandoned fiancée of her brother Edgar, now in Texas. With Lina, a teacher aware of the often precarious living conditions of her pupils, Jenny could talk openly about politics. Another friend of Jenny's at this time was the young wife of the Cologne doctor, Robert Daniels, a friend of Karl's, who ministered to the poor in the slums of Cologne. Amalie Daniels came from a respectable middle-class family and participated in the revolutionary activities of her husband only because she loved him. She was expecting her first child and asked herself whether she would have any time for the political concerns of her husband, once the baby had arrived. It was obvious to Amalie that without Lenchen's help Jenny could never have devoted herself so intensively to party work for her husband. Jenny admitted that Lenchen was a pearl, but insisted that she too took care of her house and children. The little ones were at an age when they needed their mother, especially since Jennychen and little Edgar, known as Musch, were sickly and needed special care. It was not easy to be both a mother and the secretary of the party, particularly not now, when the opposition was trying to destroy ever more openly the achievements of the revolution: freedom of speech and association.

Jenny was delighted when Karl returned from his journey and reported that he had been received with enthusiasm everywhere by revolutionary democrats. The *Neue Rheinische Zeitung* was recognized as the leading voice of the German revolution. He had received 2,000 thalers for it from Vladislav Koscielsky, the leader of Polish refugees in Berlin: otherwise the fund-raising had been disappointing. However, a counter-revolution could not be stopped by newspaper articles alone. Mass demonstrations were needed to show those in power in Berlin that the people would not surrender their hard-won freedoms.

In mid September a meeting was called by the editors of the *Neue Rheinische Zeitung* in the Franken Square in Cologne, at which 6,000 people appeared. The first speaker, Wilhelm Wolff, proposed the establishment of a committee for public safety to protect the interests of those members of the population of Cologne, who had no representatives among the existing legal authorities. This proposal was accepted with thunderous applause. The second speaker, Engels, requested that an appeal be sent to the people's assembly in Berlin with the emphatic advice that neither the Prussian Ministry nor the King had the right to dissolve the representation of the people. Should an attempt be made to do so, it was the assembly's duty to defend their places even against the force of bayonets. This proposal was also accepted unanimously.

Another mass meeting took place four days later. In the Rhine Meadows near Worringen, between Bonn and Düsseldorf, almost 10,000 people assembled and passed almost unanimously the motion of the chairman Karl Schapper that a democratic, social and red Republic should be established. And again upon the suggestion of Engels, an appeal was sent to the National Assembly in Frankfurt, stating: 'The German citizens assembled here declare that they will defend Germany with life and property, should a conflict arise between Prussia and Germany because of the opposition of the Prussian Government to the decisions of the National Assembly and of the Central Power'.[10] This formal address was also accepted with applause.

Jenny followed the procedures from her place next to the platform with lively interest. Most of the speakers she knew well; the spirited young representative of the workers in Düsseldorf, Ferdinand Lassalle, she had met only recently. He had acquired his reputation as an excellent speaker by his brilliant performance during the divorce case between Countess Hatzfeld and her husband in Berlin. There was a lot of justifiable gossip about the relationship of the Countess to her much younger attorney, and Jenny with her usual distaste for those who lived morally irregular lives, was not predisposed toward the countess, and she remained cool after she had met her, when Karl and Lassalle were working closely together.

In answer to revolutionary events in the Rhineland, several towns were declared to be in a state of siege. This caused a popular outrage and led to fierce fighting in Frankfurt, during which two hated reactionary deputies were lynched. On 25 September warrants of arrest were issued against the main speakers at the mass meetings – Engels, Wolff, Schapper, Moll and Dromke. Schapper was arrested, Engels and the others fled. When the workers wanted to erect barricades in the main square of Cologne, Marx exhorted them not to let themselves be provoked and to avoid the unequal battle against armed soldiers. They followed his advice and there was no bloodshed in Cologne. However, the commanding officer declared a state of siege on 26 September and ordered all newspapers of Cologne to cease publication. This press ban lasted two weeks.

These were weeks of extreme frustration for Karl and Jenny. The *Neue Rheinische Zeitung* was the mouthpiece of the German revolution and its non-appearance also meant serious financial loss. On 12 October, when it was permitted to appear again, Marx declared that he had only been able to overcome the financial difficulties caused by the state of siege, thanks to the help of the people of Cologne. Although most members of the editorial staff had disappeared from Cologne to escape arrest, their names still appeared on the front page of the paper. A new addition was the name of the poet Ferdinand Freiligrath, who had cursed the winds of reaction with his poem 'In Spite Of All', published in June and often quoted since. Freiligrath had earlier been arrested for his poem 'The Dead to the Living', calling upon the people to rise up in revolt. After spending four weeks in jail, he became an editor of the *Neue Rheinische Zeitung*.

During the last hectic months of 1848, the year of revolution, Jenny was constantly worried that Karl might also be arrested. 'Today I have received a summons', he wrote to Lassalle, 'and everyone thinks I'm going to be arrested tomorrow'.[11] He was accused of an offence against the press laws and was supposed to defend himself before a court of assizes in Cologne in February.

After a *coup d'état* in Prussia, the people's assembly was moved from Berlin to Brandenburg in November, leading to protest meetings everywhere. The Rhenish District Committee of Democrats of all democratic societies urged the population to refuse paying taxes and thus force the government to recognize the people's assembly again. The *Neue Rheinische Zeitung* endorsed this demand and published the slogan 'No More Taxes' on its front page for a month.

The authorities in Berlin considered this a further proof that Marx was a dangerous demagogue and had to be silenced. However, Marx was so occupied with the daily changing events that he had no time to reflect about his own future. There were nights when Jenny hardly saw him, for apart from his journalistic work, he had to take part in meetings, give speeches and lead discussions, since he had become the President of the Cologne Workers' Union. Besides, he had to collect money for his arrested or escaped associates, which was not easy, for his family too needed money. Here Jenny had to help. She got some support from her mother or went to a pawnshop and got some money for her silver. But it was not the often scarce housekeeping money that worried her, for Lenchen always found some means of getting bread and vegetables. What really worried Jenny was the health of her children Jennychen and Musch. Both were susceptible to any change in weather and often had fever and little appetite. Lenchen recommended that they eat lots of fruit, but fruit was scarce in winter. Jenny got nuts and dried fruit from her mother, who also sent her the traditional Christmas goose and presents for the children. In spite of the gloomy political situation that appeared on the horizon at the end of this year of revolution which had begun so promisingly, the mood in the Marx house was full of expectation: Karl and Jenny greeted the new year with a champagne toast on the victory of the revolution.

III

On New Year's Day Karl read aloud to Jenny from the *Neue Rheinische Zeitung*'s leading article, 'The Revolutionary Movement':

> The defeat of the working class in France meant also the suppression of those nationalities which had answered the call of the Gallic cock with heroic attempts at emancipation. But once again Poland, Italy and Ireland were ravaged, raped, assassinated by Prussian, Austrian and English policemen . . . The defeat of the working class in France, the victory of the French bourgeoisie was also the victory of the East over the West, the defeat of civilization by barbarism. In Wallachia the Russians and their puppets, the Turks, started the oppression of the Romance nations, in Vienna Croats, Pandours, Czechs, Circassians and similar rabble strangled German freedom and at this moment the Czar is all powerful in Europe . . . Hence the slogan of European liberation is the emancipation of the working class. [12]

England was the rock upon which the waves of revolution foundered, England was the country that had dominated the world with its industry and transformed whole nations into its proletarians. Any attempt at a national–economic revolutionary change would be a storm in a teacup without England. A world war would be necessary to break the power of the English bourgeoisie and to liberate their oppressed proletarians. To Jenny's question about what she could expect in the coming year, the editor-in-chief of the *Neue Rheinische Zeitung* answered briefly and clearly: 'Revolutionary revolt of the French workers, world war – that is the content of the year 1849.'[13]

The weeks that followed were hectic enough, even without a world war. Throughout Europe there were revolutionary uprisings, often suppressed by brutal military force. The *Neue Rheinische Zeitung* protested fiercely against the violation of the rights given to the people, and when in February Marx had to appear before the court of assizes in Cologne to defend himself against the charge of 'incitement to rebellion', he did it so convincingly that he was acquitted. Jenny was very proud of him. In the presence of hundreds of curious observers both inside and outside the courtroom, she heard how Karl cleverly reversed the accusation. In the best style of Hegelian dialectics, the accused became the accuser. Not he but the King and his ministers were to blame for the violation of the constitution. 'By the cancellation of the constitution given in March, the Crown made a revolution and cast aside the existing legal conditions. It cannot appeal to laws that it has so shamefully overturned.'[14] It was the right, indeed the duty, of the press to undermine the conditions created by the breach of the constitution. The suppression of freedom of expression was a sign of despotism, and it was the right of all citizens to fight against it.

After this loudly applauded speech for which the president of the court thanked Marx, the latter left the court a free man. A group of Cologne workers met him in the street and led him triumphantly back to his office, where he was greeted by Jenny and his associates as a victor over reaction.

But the months of March and April brought less happy events. On the night of 2 March two officers from the

Cologne garrison appeared in their apartment and ordered Marx to name the author of an article about a certain officer that had caused anger in the highest quarters. Jenny was not surprised that he refused to co-operate, and she was impressed by the way he forced them to leave by accusing them of a breach of domestic peace. Such an event made her anxious to keep him close at hand, and she was therefore terrified when he told her that he had to undertake another journey through North Germany and Westphalia in order to save the paper that was once again financially threatened and to sound out the revolutionary situation. During this journey he was shadowed by the police, for Berlin had become convinced that Marx must be stopped. King Frederick William IV personally ordered the Prussian detective Wilhelm Stieber to take counter-measures against the communist conspiracies.

When Marx returned in May, he warned Jenny that the family should be prepared for yet another expulsion. The counter-revolution had been victorious in Prussia and was about to pacify the other German states by force. He showed his scorn in a long article about *The Deeds of the House of Hohenzollern*: 'The Prussians are once again as before, a Vice-Kingdom under Russian domination; Hohenzollern is again subject to the autocrat of all Russians, and lord over all the small boyards of Saxony, Bavaria, Hessen-Homburg, Waldeck etc . . .'[15]

Moreover, various inflammatory articles convinced Berlin that the *Neue Rheinische Zeitung* had crossed the Rubicon and was now propagating armed uprisings. But since there was a fear that the official prohibition of the paper would lead to further unrest in the Rhineland, it was decided that the same purpose could be achieved by expelling its editor-in-chief, and Marx duly received an expulsion order on 16 May 1849, requiring him 'to leave the country within 24 hours'.[16]

Although the one day's notice was not to be taken literally and Marx stayed in Germany till the end of May the following days were a time of desperate worry for him and his family. The editorial office of the *Neue Rheinische Zeitung* had to be

shut down, the printing machines sold, and fellow-workers
and printers paid. Last but not least, a final edition of the paper
was brought out, printed in flaming red letters. It appeared
on 19 May with a poem on the front page in the spirit of
Freiligrath:

> Hold up your head in spite of all that's bad:
> With scorn on my lips in an angry tone,
> My sword held high in my hand
> While dying still shouting: Rebellion!
> Thus was my noble end . . .[17]

Then Marx went to Paris; Engels, under warrant of arrest by
the Prussian government, joined the revolutionary army in
the Palatinate and as Willich's adjutant took part in fighting in
Baden and the Palatinate; Jenny, Lenchen and the children
travelled to Trier to her mother. On the way there they stayed
a week at Bingen, where they met the journalist Heinzen, who
was scorned by Karl and married to an elegant actress. In
Frankfurt, Jenny, short of money as always, pawned some
silver which she had only recently redeemed from the Brussels
pawnbroker.

Her reception in Trier was different from the almost triumphal one of the year before. Then she had been the wife of the
leader of a revolutionary movement about to take over power
in the state; now she was the wife of an outlawed refugee. Her
mother was particularly mortified by this development, for
she had hoped that out of love for Jenny and his children Karl
would give up his revolutionary activities, and continue with
his promising journalistic career. But he had failed for the
second time. Meanwhile her stepson Ferdinand von Westphalen was making a brilliant career for himself in the Prussian
civil service and there were rumours that the King had singled
him out for promotion. Compared with the respectable and
successful lives of her three stepchildren, those of her own
children were markedly unsuccessful – Edgar had failed in
Texas and come home, while Jenny and her children were

facing a dark future. Her own small fortune was insufficient to provide for her daughter and her grandchildren. No wonder Caroline worried.

Jenny worried too, but to her mother and her Trier acquaintances she maintained a veneer of calm confidence. In letters to her friend Lina Schöler, she admitted: 'Life is not a bed of roses here, I can tell you that, dear, faithful Lina'.[18] Since her arrival in Trier, 'the smallest, meanest nest filled with gossip and ridiculous self-satisfaction',[19] she had not breathed freely. And in her heart, heavy with sorrow and longing,

lies the anxiety about my dear husband. You can imagine, how afraid I was, when I heard about the revolt in Paris. The terrible cholera raging there, kept me in constant fear. And in addition the general, heavy sorrows and defeats of our party, the difficult situation facing all who fought for the principle of a new world. Even the thought that my dear Karl has so far come through all dangers worries me. I always fear that he may have to endure greater and more terrible torments and am completely at a loss to know what lies ahead of us. My dear Karl remains confident and cheerful and considers all the pressures that we have to endure only heralds of a coming and complete victory of our view of life. So far he has been unquestioned in Paris and he wants to remain there and have us join him. But should he not feel safe anymore, then Geneva would be the next place to emigrate to. I would like that. I would like to spend the few months of summer in such a heavenly, natural environment. I am hoping to receive definite travel orders in the next letter.[20]

The travel orders that soon came were not for Geneva, but Paris. After taking tearful leave of her mother, who asked herself anxiously whether she would ever see her prodigal daughter again, she journeyed to Paris with Lenchen and the children, where she was received by Karl in a small but expensive apartment in the rue de Lille. She requested Lina to send her books and furniture from Trier to Paris, but not to the apartment in town, for she had found a cheaper one in the suburbs. However, four days later Marx was informed by the French authorities that his permission to stay in Paris was cancelled and he was exiled to the Morbihan, a marshy, godforsaken region of Brittany.

Marx protested vehemently against this 'disguised assassination attempt', as he called the expulsion order, and informed Engels that he would emigrate to England and publish a German paper in London. He counted on Engels' co-operation.

What was to happen to his family, he did not know. Jenny, Lenchen and the children should of course join him in London. But how? There was no money for the crossing. Jenny again had to ask her mother for help, though her mother was becoming increasingly impatient with her daughter's vagabond life. And she did not even know that Jenny was six months' pregnant and expecting her fourth child in November. Marx urged Jenny to pawn some of her silver in Paris. He left France on 24 August; Jenny was to follow him to England three weeks later. Once again it was her job to find the money for the journey somehow.

She discovered that Paris, in spite of the revolution a few months earlier, again showed its old sparkle. 'Aristocracy and bourgeoisie are feeling safe after the unfortunate 13 June and the new victories of their party. By the 14th all the great men, who had gone into hiding, came out of their hiding places, plus their coaches and servants, and there is splendour and magnificence in the bright streets of Paris.'[21] She left the continent with a heavy heart. With the unfailing help of Lenchen, she succeeded in settling her financial affairs by the middle of September and boarded a Channel steamer in Calais. When the chalk cliffs of Dover loomed up, she looked longingly for her husband. But Karl had not come to receive his exiled family. 'Georg Weerth met me, when I arrived in London sick and exhausted with my three little persecuted children.'[22]

The tone of sadness that vibrates through this sentence would dominate the next and bleakest chapter in Jenny's life.

8

The Hells of London

In the first days after her arrival in London Jenny and her family found lodgings in Leicester Square, a meeting-place for German refugees. She had learned English from her father as a child, but she hardly needed it when she got to London. In the streets and squares around her lodgings German and French were spoken as much as English. Soho, the quarter of London that was to become her home for years, offered refuge to thousands of expelled European revolutionaries, who had come to England, the most advanced capitalist country of the world, because it was the only country that offered asylum to every political refugee.

Relief committees were set up to alleviate the worst poverty among the refugees. They turned for help to friends and relatives in their homelands. The social–democratic relief committee in London, presided over by Marx and Engels, appealed to the party in Germany with a request to send funds to prevent comrades, who had fought for the honour and freedom of their German fatherland, from begging for bread on the street-corners of London.

While her husband was occupied with such time-consuming relief activities and also editing with Engels a political–economic journal intended as a continuation of the *Neue Rheinische Zeitung*, Jenny installed herself in a small house in Chelsea and awaited the arrival of her fourth child.

On 5 November – the day on which the English commemorate Guy Fawkes' conspiracy to blow up the Houses of
Parliament – Jenny gave birth to a boy, whom they named
Heinrich, in memory of Karl's father, but who immediately
acquired the nickname 'Föxchen', in memory of the day of his
birth. Jenny had to nurse the child herself because English wet-
nurses were too expensive. 'But the poor little angel drank in
so much worry and quiet sorrow that he was always sickly,
suffering great pain day and night. He has never slept a night
since his birth, two or three hours at most. Lately he has also
had violent cramps. The poor child has been teetering constantly between death and a miserable life. He suckled so
fiercely in his pains that my breasts became sore and broke
open; blood often streamed into his poor, trembling little
mouth',[1] wrote Jenny to Weydemeyer. She goes on to depict
movingly the misery of her refugee existence:

> One day, as I was sitting at home, our concierge suddenly came
> in; we had paid her more than 250 thalers in the course of the
> winter and had signed a contract to pay the rest of the money not
> to her but directly to the landlord, who had garnished her accounts
> at an earlier time. On the day she came in, she denied there was a
> contract and demanded the £5 that we still owed her. Since we did
> not have them at the moment . . . two bailiffs entered, impounded
> all my few possessions, beds, linen, clothes, everything, even the
> cradle of my poor child and the best toys of my girls, who wept
> bitter tears. They threatened to take everything within two hours
> – I had to lie on the bare floor with my freezing children, my sore
> breasts . . . The next day we had to leave the house, it was cold
> and rainy, my husband is trying to find a house for us, but no one
> wants to have us when they hear we have four children. Finally, a
> friend helps us, we pay and I quickly sell all my beds to pay the
> chemist, baker, butcher and milkman who come rushing up to
> me with their bills because our pawning scandal had made them
> suspicious. The beds are taken outside the house and loaded onto a
> cart – what happens? It was long after sunset, when English law
> forbids such actions, the landlord appears with constables, claims
> that some of his things could be on the cart and that we wanted to
> escape and go to another country. In less than five minutes, more

Jenny von Westphalen

Caroline von Westphalen, Jenny's mother

Ludwig von Westphalen, Jenny's father

Top left: Jenny as a teenager.   *Top right:* Jenny as a young wife.   *Bottom left:* Edgar von Westphalen, Jenny's brother.   *Bottom right:* Ferdinand von Westphalen, Jenny's half-brother

Friedrich Engels and Karl Marx with his three daughters Jenny, Eleanor, and Laura

Top left: Eleanor Marx, the youngest daughter. *Top right:* Laura Marx, the second daughter. *Bottom left:* Jenny, the eldest daughter. *Bottom right:* Edgar 'Musch' Marx, Marx's son, at the age of three, and a letter from him to his mother

Jenny's birthplace in Salzwedel

Top left: The Marx family's London flat, in Dean Street, where they lived from May 1850 to October 1856. *Top right:* Helene Demuth, the faithful 'Lenchen', housekeeper with the Marx family from 1845. *Bottom left:* Grafton Terrace, the Marx family's second London home, where they lived from October 1856. *Bottom right:* 1 Modena Villas, the Marx family's third London house, where they lived from March 1864 than two to three hundred people are standing open-mouthed before our door, the whole mob of Chelsea. The beds are carried back in, they can only be handed over to the buyer the next morning after sunrise. When I had been able to pay every penny, after selling all our personal possessions, I moved with my little darlings into our present small two rooms in the German Hotel, 1 Leicester Street, Leicester Square where we met with a human reception for £5 10s. a week.[2]

But even there they could not stay long. One morning the innkeeper appeared, refused to bring them breakfast and told them to leave his hotel at once. Thanks to some financial help she received just in time from her mother, Jenny and her children found two rooms in the house of a Jewish lace-dealer, 'where we struggled hard all through the summer'.[3]

While his family tried to cope somehow with daily life, Marx worked tirelessly organizing and propagating his communist ideas. His battle cry was: 'The Permanent Revolution'. He wrote pages and pages of articles about it for his *Neue Rheinische Zeitung Political Economy Review* which was published in Hamburg, and of which four single numbers and one double appeared between March and November 1850.

Together with Engels, he organized the Communist League, sent emissaries to Germany, France, Switzerland and even to America, to make propaganda for the League and to collect money for German refugees in England. He wrote polemic articles against the representatives of the German petit-bourgeois democrats, such as Gottfried Kinkel, and put up every homeless party comrade. This often led to unpleasant surprises, as when the former Prussian Lieutenant August Willich arrived in London after his adventures in the Palatinate free corps and, as Jenny said, 'settled in with us as a communist *frère et compagnon.* He appeared in our bedroom early in the morning, a real Don Quixote in a grey woollen jacket and, instead of a belt, a red cloth around his waist and tried, with Prussian horse-laughs, to hold forth at length about "natural" communism. But Karl made short work of his effort. And he did not fare any better with me when he tried to wheedle out the worm that is in every marriage.'[4]

With the hoped-for royalty income from the *political-economic* review arriving only occasionally and scantily, the financial condition of the family became increasingly precarious. Jenny addressed further appeals for help to her mother and to friends like Weydemeyer, the leader of the Frankfurt Communist League. She implored him to send the money from the magazine immediately to London, where it was urgently needed for her hungry family.

Marx meanwhile, in co-operation with English Chartists and French socialists, founded a world-league of revolutionary communists in April 1850, with the aim of overthrowing all classes and of subjugating them to the dictatorship of the proletariat. The participants in such conspiratorial meetings, which took place on the first floor of 20 Windmill Street in Soho, were reliable party comrades who took an oath to keep all party affairs secret. Police spies nevertheless managed to infiltrate the meetings.

Among the Prussian authorities with an interest in the activities of the London German communists, it was the Minister of the Interior, Ferdinand von Westphalen, Jenny's half-brother, who particularly wanted to know what his brother-in-law was doing. He therefore sent to London a crack agent, Wilhelm Stieber, who later became the chief of Bismarck's secret service. Stieber arrived in London as a newspaper editor called Schmidt, allegedly to visit the Great Exhibition. After succeeding in the infiltration of German communist meetings, he sent a long report to Berlin, in which he states that under Marx's chairmanship even regicide was discussed: 'in a meeting the day before yesterday, where Marx and Wolff were chairmen, one of the participants shouted: "The mooncalf will not escape her fate. English steel is the best steel in the world, and the guillotine is waiting for every crowned head".'[5]

Since the expression 'mooncalf' obviously referred to Queen Victoria, the Prussian Minister Otto von Manteuffel informed the British ambassador in Berlin of the high treason being plotted a few hundred yards from Buckingham Palace. As a result, discussions took place in the British parliament concerning the 'Alien Bill', a law first passed in 1793 and again in 1848 which permitted the government to expel undesirable aliens at any time.

In view of the danger that he might be expelled from England, Marx addressed an open letter to the editor of *The Spectator*, requesting space to publish an article that he and Engels had written about Prussian spies in London. He makes it known in this piece that he has been watched by police spies day and night for a week: 'Not only are the doors of the house we live in watched by more than dubious-looking individuals, who impertinently take notes when anyone enters or leaves, but we cannot take a single step without being followed by them. We cannot ride an omnibus or enter a café without being honoured by the company of at least one of these unknown friends'.[6] He concludes with an appeal to the honourable English tradition that eschewed the system of police informers customary in all other countries of Europe. Although the British government made no attempt to expel Marx, it kept an eye on him and his party, and twenty-five years later it would reject Marx's request for British citizenship.

Berlin watched the events in London with alarm, for according to Stieber's report: 'The party will begin with the guillotine and end with a tabula rasa. It is so unusually dangerous for the state, the family and the social order that all governments and every citizen should join forces against this invisible lurking enemy and not rest, if for nothing else than the instinct of self-preservation, until the last fibre of this cancer has been eradicated with fire and sword.'[7]

As a result of this report the Prussian authorities began a witch hunt which led to the arrest of a number of members of the Marx Party who were living in Germany, and finally to the famous Cologne Communist Trial of 4 October 1852.

During these years of constant political battling, the personal situation of the leader of the movement was often hopeless. Marx lived with his four children, Jenny and Lenchen in a dingy attic apartment: seven people in two rooms without running water. The Prussian agent reported:

Marx lives in one of the worst and hence cheapest quarters of London. He has two rooms, the one with the view of the street being the drawing-room, behind it the bedroom. There is not one piece of good, solid furniture in the entire flat. Everything is broken, tattered and torn, finger-thick dust everywhere, and everything in the greatest disorder; a large, old fashioned table, covered with waxcloth, stands in the middle of the drawing-room, on it lie manuscripts, books, newspapers, then the children's toys, bits and pieces of the woman's sewing things, next to it a few teacups with broken rims, dirty spoons, knives, forks, candle-sticks, inkpot, glasses, dutch clay pipes, tobacco-ash, in a word all kinds of trash, and everything on one table; a junk dealer would be ashamed of it. When you enter the Marx flat your sight is dimmed by coal and tobacco smoke so that you grope around at first as if you were in a cave, until your eyes get used to these fumes and, as in a fog, you gradually notice a few objects. Everything is dirty, everything covered with dust; it is dangerous to sit down. Here is a chair with only three legs, there the children play kitchen on another chair that happens to be whole; true – it is offered to the visitor, but the children's kitchen is not removed; if you sit on it you risk a pair of trousers. But nothing of this embarrasses Marx or his wife in the least; you are received in the friendliest manner, are cordially offered a pipe, tobacco and whatever else there is; a spirited conversation makes up for the domestic defects and in the end you become reconciled because of the company, find it interesting, even original. This is the faithful portrait of the family life of the communist leader Marx.[8]

What is lacking in this report is any attempt to understand the state of mind of the main characters. Was Jenny's constant indisposition a reaction of her body to an environment so alien to her nature and upbringing? She travelled to Holland in August 1850, in spite of her concern about her sick child, in order to seek help from Karl's uncle, Lion Philips. She was already pregnant again 'and anticipated the birth of a fifth child and the future with despair'.[9] When she arrived after a stormy crossing and 'fifteen hours of terrible sea-sickness, tired and apprehensive',[10] she noted to her horror, that Karl's uncle did not recognize her. 'I got the familiar hug only after I had introduced myself'.[11] And that is all that she did get. When she indicated that unless he would help them now,

> we had no other choice but to go to America, he replied that he thought this was very sensible, if there was something positive for you to do there . . . I am afraid, dear Karl, I am coming home to you, quite empty-handed, disappointed, torn apart and tortured by a fear of death. Oh, if you knew how much I am longing for you and the little ones. I cannot write anything about the children, my eyes begin to tremble and I must remain strong. So kiss them, kiss the little angels a thousand times for me. I know that you and Lenchen will take good care of them. Without Lenchen I would not have any peace of mind here.[12]

Jenny would have been less fulsome in her praises for Lenchen had she known what Lenchen and Karl were doing while she was away in Holland: it was very probably at this time that Lenchen conceived a child by him.

At her departure Uncle Philips gave Jenny a small, personal present for her youngest child, but he did not notice with what a heavy heart she left him. 'I came home with despair in my heart. My poor little Edgar came running toward me with his friendly face and my Föxchen stretched out his little arms toward me. I was not to have his caresses much longer. The delicate child died of cramps, the result of pneumonia. I suffered great pain. It was the first child I lost. I had no idea then, what other sufferings I had to endure that made everything meaningless.'[13]

9

Death Street

Dean Street, in the centre of London, where the Marx family spent the first hard years of their English existence, was for Jenny synonymous with distress and death. She lost three children during these years and with these children her joy in life and strength of mind. Here stood the cliffs upon which, as Marx said, 'her life was wrecked'.

The narrow, three-storey house in the Georgian style, number 28, still stands today. An Italian restaurant is found on its ground floor; the garret and the two rooms in the attic are empty and are shown to visitors who want to gain some impression of where and how the chief ideologist of the communist movement lived. A memorial plaque with the inscription 'Here lived Karl Marx' was put up in August 1967 at the instigation of the London correspondent of *Pravda*. But to get an understanding of the living conditions of the Marx family one must compare today's empty and cleanly swept rooms, with the description by Stieber given in the previous chapter.

We know that at times eight people lived in this miserably furnished two-room attic that belonged to an Irishman named Kavanaugh, who rented it to Marx for £22 a year. Eight people: four adults – Karl, Jenny, Lenchen and a nurse – and four children worked, ate and slept together. There was no lavatory, bath or running water. It was easier for Lenchen to bear this kind of life than for Jenny, 'the sister of the Prussian Minister von Westphalen, a cultured and charming lady, who has accustomed herself to this gypsy life out of love for her husband and seems to feel quite at home in this misery'.[1]

What Stieber says here is not true. Jenny never felt at home in such misery. She was often so desperate that she told her husband: she wished 'she were in the grave with her children'.[2] The first years in England were also years of disappointed hopes for Marx. After the failure of his journalistic career in Cologne, he tried to start a new one in London. But his attempt to gain a livelihood for himself and his family and a mouthpiece for his political ideas by publishing, jointly with Engels, the *Political-Economic Review* also failed. The fourth and last number of the magazine appeared in October and in spite of Jenny's desperate cries for help they did not receive much money from it.

Engels, who realized that he could not make a living as a journalist in England, sadly decided to go back to Manchester and join his father's firm, even though he was convinced that the capitalist system he would support by this move was about to collapse. This also put him in the position of being able to subsidize Marx's resources. Jenny wrote to him that she was glad he was leaving London and about to become 'a great Cotton Lord'.[3] In his reply Engels said: 'As to the Cotton Lord, I don't know, my old man doesn't want me here longer than absolutely necessary.'[4] However, for the time being he had a job and a steady income.

Marx missed his friend's presence the more since he had completely fallen out with all his former followers. Battle-tried comrades like Schapper and Willich were convinced that European workers could be moved much more easily by appeals to direct revolutionary action than by learned treatises about labour and capital. They scorned 'journalistic characters' in the communist movement, who believed that revolutions could be 'scientifically proven'. Marx, who only a short while ago had been at the centre of the revolutionary movement, was suddenly the only member of his party in England, a party that on the continent was still severely persecuted by the Prussian police. There was, in addition, his domestic misery and Jenny's deep despair about the death of her little Föxchen. She could not get out of her mind the thought that the child was a victim of their living conditions and that he would not have died if he had had better care. In her autobiographical essay, written twenty years later, she observes: 'The years 1851–52 were for us the years of the greatest and at the same time pettiest worries, torments, disappointments and privations of all kinds'.[5]

Among Jenny's greatest disappointments was an event in the early summer of 1851 which, she says, 'I do not want to touch on more closely, but which added greatly to the increase of our inner and outer worries'.[6] This event, not elaborated upon, was the birth of another child – but not hers. She had given birth to her own fifth, a girl named Franziska, in the family bedroom in Dean Street on 28 March. And three months later in the same room her faithful Lenchen was delivered of a boy, entered in the registry of births as Frederick Demuth. Marx found the view of two pregnant women in his narrow flat tragi-comic, but Jenny did not, for Lenchen gave no answer when asked who the father of her child was. In desperation Jenny turned to her husband. Though Karl said nothing directly, he hinted that the philanderer Engels probably was the man. In April he travelled to Manchester to explain to Engels a '*mystère*' that he had mentioned in his letter but did not want to write about. He convinced Engels that it was in the interest of the party for Engels to acknowledge the paternity of Lenchen's child. Engels, who had no children of his own, agreed but declared that he personally did not want to have anything to do with the child.

However, as far as Jenny was concerned, the matter was not settled. She urged Lenchen to be honest. But she remained silent, finally deciding that the best way to solve the whole problem was to leave the Marx household. In Jenny's letter to Born, mentioned earlier, she added 'the sad news, but with indignation between the lines, that her faithful and untiring maid, who was practically a member of the family, had left her'.[7]

But Marx protested against that. Lenchen's flight would look like a confession of guilt and damage her reputation as well as his. The best solution was to give up the child to an English family for adoption. We can only guess at Lenchen's feelings about this proposal, which was carried out. We know from many accounts of Jenny's daughters that she was very fond of children. Her will proves that she loved her son, whom she could see only secretly, up to the end of her life: for when she died in 1890, nine years after Jenny, she left him the entirety of her modest fortune.

She knew, of course, who Frederick's father was, but she also knew that an illegitimate child could not be educated together with the legitimate children of the head of the Marx Party. If she wanted to keep her son, she would have to leave the Marx family. But that was practically impossible, for how should she take care of herself and her child, not to mention the fact that Marx was not only the father of her child, but the man she loved? She was the only person before whom the fearless fighter for a better world order trembled. 'It has been said that nobody is a great man to his valet. To Lenchen Marx was certainly not great. But she would have died for him',[8] according to Liebknecht.

The suspicion and then the certainty that Karl was the father of Lenchen's child was a hard blow for Jenny. She had left her family and fatherland out of love for him, she was sharing the hopeless misery of his refugee existence out of love for him, helped him with his work and was always at his side when he needed her. Karl too loved and needed her, but he was a man forced by circumstances to live in the closest proximity with two women, both of whom loved him. Whenever one was gone, the other was present. The temptations were obvious. In the end Jenny silently accepted a *ménage a trois*, although it hurt her. And Lenchen, obliged to keep her relationship to Marx a secret while she lived, was allowed to lie in the same grave with him and Jenny.

During the time of Lenchen's approaching confinement, Marx fled into the solitude of the reading room of the British Museum, perhaps partly because of guilt feelings or because he could not bear to watch Jenny's sadness. But his work on a study of capitalist economics required extensive research which could only be carried out in a library. Every morning about 9 o'clock he left the flat in Dean Street and returned home only in the evening, sometimes after midnight, at the end of an extensive pub-crawl down Tottenham Court Road with youthful admirers like Liebknecht. He left Lenchen with the responsibility for his three children and his ailing wife. She also had to find money for food for the family, which often meant a visit to the pawnbroker; once she even pawned her master's shoes.

The only ray of light in these gloomy years was an inquiry from Charles Anderson Dana, the editor of the *New York Daily Tribune*, asking Marx whether he wanted to become the European correspondent of this, the largest American newspaper. The fee for an article was £1 and the paper was interested in two articles a week. The idea of a regular income made Jenny and Lenchen absolutely rapturous and Marx quickly accepted Dana's offer, although his knowledge of English was not yet good enough to write formal articles. However, Marx was sure that Engels would do him this good turn, too. And he was right. Every week Engels sent him one or two articles from Manchester, which Marx redirected from London to New York and for which he received the promised fee. It was often not easy for Engels to find the time to write these articles: 'I am sitting here up to my ears in work. Eleven business letters lie on my desk which I still have to write today and it is almost 7 o'clock. However, I will concoct an article for Dana, if possible tonight but at the latest by tomorrow evening.'[9]

How urgently the American money was needed in the Marx household is shown in a letter from Jenny to Weydemeyer, who had emigrated to New York. She begged him to 'urge Dana to name a house in London, where we can collect the fees more quickly'[10] for people in America do not know 'how everything is hanging by a thread here and to get 10s. at the right time can save us from a terrible predicament.'[11] How terrible the situation was Jenny reveals in the review of her life, when she describes the death of her one-year-old daughter Franziska:

> At Easter of the same year, 1852, our poor little Franziska fell sick with a severe case of bronchitis. For three days the poor child fought for her life, suffering very much. Her poor, lifeless body rested in the little garret room, all we others moved into the front room, and when night came we made our beds on the floor and our three living children lay next to us and we wept for the little angel who was resting cold and dead near us. The death of our dear child happened at the time of our most abject poverty. Our German friends were not able to help us at that moment . . . With fear in my heart I ran to a French refugee, who lived near us and had visited us. He gave me at once £2 with deep sympathy, and the little coffin, in which my poor child now rests in peace, was paid for with them. She had no cradle when she came into the world and even her last home was long in coming.[12]

The death of his second child in less than a year also depressed Marx and increased his hatred of the bourgeoisie, whom he held responsible for the 'shit' in which he was stuck. With the feeling of being a slave, bound to the iron law of the bourgeois market of supply and demand, Marx worked desperately 'amidst children's noises and the domestic hustle and bustle'[13] on his *Eighteenth Brumaire*, a long critical essay about the *coup d'état* of Louis Napoleon, that Jenny copied and sent to New York. Marx hoped that it would appear in the journal *Die Revolution* which Weydemeyer had founded. It did appear, but only much later and yielded, as Jenny remarked, 'less than nothing'.

The sensational Communist Trial of Cologne of 4 October 1852, in which a number of members of the Marx Party, accused by the Prussian government of high treason, had to defend themselves, was a time of hectic activity for Marx and his family, but it was another period when less than nothing came in. Jenny's support for the cause was no less whole-hearted because it was a fight hopelessly carried on against the entire power of the Prussian State, embodied in the person of her half-brother Ferdinand.

The ring-leader in this campaign was the Prussian police agent Stieber, who had visited Marx under an assumed name and had personally received from Marx a copy of 'the red-bound book entitled "The Programme of the Communist League".'[14] When Stieber asked who the members of this League were, Marx – 'a stocky, middle-aged man in a shabby coat with stiff shirtfront and wavy black hair and beard, a university professor in appearance. His only striking feature was a penetrating glance under an extremely high forehead, furthermore a loosely waving neck-scarf of the kind that artists, painters etc. used to wear, also a sparkling monocle that he wore inserted in the socket of his right eye'[15] – Marx answered that the central register of the League was deposited with a certain Dietz, whose address he gave Stieber. Having found out the whereabouts of the list, Stieber was about to leave. But Marx would not let him go. 'He seemed to want to test me further: "Are you an editor", he asked me.'[16] When Stieber answered that he was really a would-be physician, who had been expelled from the university because of his revolutionary convictions, Marx replied: ' "So you are a phy-sician. Then tell me, please, what is an effective medicine against haemorrhoidal pain?" I thought at first I had mis-understood him, but Marx explained without embarrassment that he was suffering intolerably from this disease which made it such a torture to sit down to write, that he could now only work while standing up'.[17]

Marx did not know that he himself had given Stieber – whom he called a liar and forger of documents in his 'Revel-ations of the Communist Trial in Cologne' – the material for the indictment. And Jenny realized that it was a battle between her husband and the Prussian state, for during the course of the trial Marx was held responsible for everything, for all the revolutions of 1848. 'The battle against this official power, that is equipped with money and means, is of course quite interesting and the more glorious for us, if we should win it, since they have everything, money and power, while we often do not know where to get the paper on which to write letters'.[18]

The Cologne Communist Trial did not end with a victory for Marx, but during the five weeks' legal proceedings the German public learned, by means of the secret messages that Marx knew how to get to the accused from London, about the dubious methods practised by the Prussian police under Stieber's administration, to procure proofs for the presumed acts of high treason committed by the accused. The members of the jury rejected the assertion that everybody who had a copy of *The Communist Manifesto* in his possession was a traitor. Nevertheless, most of the accused received prison sentences of from three to five years.

A regular office was established at Marx's flat during the trial: 'Two or three write, some run around, others scrape pennies together to assure the continued existence of the writers in order to prove the unheard-of scandal of the old, official world. And in between it my three cheerful children sing and whistle and are often sharply called to order by their papa. What tomfoolery it all is!'[19]

The three children – Jennychen, Laura and Musch – were indeed their consolation for the dreary everyday life of their London refugee existence. Jenny and Lenchen watched over them with motherly care and Karl indulged them as best he could, letting them play on his back, while sitting at his wobbly table writing articles, and romping around with them during their Sunday excursions to Hampstead Heath. Much as he loved his two girls, his greatest hope was his son, for he considered men more valuable than women in the age of revolutions. And still he was often quite unable to provide for them. 'For the last eight to ten days I have been able to feed my family with bread and potatotes, but it is questionable, whether I can get anything today . . . How can I cope with all this devil's shit?'[20] he asked Engels.

Illness was the consequence of this poor diet. There was hardly a day when not one member of the family was ailing: 'My wife is sick, Jennychen is sick, Lenchen has a kind of nervous complaint. But I cannot and could not call the doctor, because I have no money for medicine',[21] such was the refrain in the weekly letters to Engels that always culminated in the request that his friend should immediately send a few pounds – which Engels did whenever he was able, although his own means were scarce enough. Conditions improved somewhat later when Marx was able to write English articles himself for the New York paper.

Jenny writes that the Christmas of 1853, the fifth since their arrival in London, was the first cheerful festival they had celebrated. 'The hard, daily gnawing worries had been overcome by Karl's connection with the "Tribune". The children have been romping around all summer in the open, in the parks. We had cherries, strawberries and even grapes this year and our friends brought the dear trio all kinds of pretty presents. They got dolls, guns and kitchenware and drums and trumpets, and Dronke came late in the evening to decorate the Christmas tree. It was such a happy evening.'[22] But, as ever in Jenny's life, the shadow of misfortune was soon cast over this happy moment. 'A week later the first traces of that disastrous disease that would carry him off a year later appeared in our dear Edgar[23] . . . If we had been able to leave our small, unhealthy flat and take the child to the seashore – perhaps we could have saved him.'[24]

The course of the following years in the small flat in Dean Street was tragic. A mortally ill child of seven clung to life in a family from which death was never far. Jenny was pregnant for the sixth time, while her beloved Musch was wrestling with death. The idea of giving birth to yet another child in such a hopeless environment made her so sick that Marx was seriously worried about her life. 'The condition of my wife is dangerous',[25] he wrote to Engels; and since he could not do his own work because of these domestic worries, he sighed in Latin: *Beatus ille* = happy is he, who has no family'.[26] He added sarcastically that he seemed to be much better at making children than money.

Jenny's sixth child in her twelve-year marriage was born on 16 January 1855. It was again a girl. 'Unfortunately', Marx thought, for 'if it were male, it would be better'.[27] The child was called Eleanor, but – like all members of the Marx family – was nicknamed, this one being called 'Tussy'. While Lenchen took care of the lively new baby, Jenny and Karl worried about the life of their son Edgar. The boy was obviously suffering great pain from what the doctor called abdominal sclerosis – but he kept his good humour and even sang with a loud voice the words from Freiligrath's version of the Marseillaise:

> Oh, come June, come and bring us deeds
> my heart is longing for brave deeds . . .[28]

But even before June came, Musch's life – Engels called him 'Colonel Musch' in tribute to his courage – was nearing its end. Torn between hope and despair, his parents watched his struggle with death: 'Musch has been getting better in the last days and the doctor is hopeful'[29] Marx informed Engels on 27 March 1855. But three days later the disease took on 'the character of an abdominal consumption, hereditary in our family, and even the doctors seem to have given up hope. For a whole week my wife has been as ill as never before from mental exhaustion. And my heart is bleeding and my head burning.'[30] On Good Friday, between five and six o'clock, their beloved Musch died in the arms of his father. 'It is indescribable how much we miss the child. I have suffered all kinds of bad luck, but I know only now what real misfortune is. I feel broken down. Fortunately I have had such terrible headaches since the funeral that I have not been able to think, hear or see anything.'[31]

And Jenny was at the end of her strength, for death had taken from her 'the best loved being I had in the world, my dear, only Edgar. It is a pain that never heals, never becomes a scar – because neither wound nor scar will heal – the wound is in the deepest, quiet heart, where it will never get old and stop bleeding.'[32] She did not know how she could go on living in these desolate rooms, where cradle and coffin stood side by side. And Marx decided to leave the flat in Dean Street for a few weeks, after Musch – as Foxchen and Franziska before him – had been buried in the Tottenham Court Road cemetery. With Jenny, about whose peace of mind he was greatly worried, he went to visit Engels in Manchester.

When they returned home, they were again met by the familiar daily misery – bills from bakers, butchers, greengrocers, milkmen that had to be paid, demands for the rent and the high doctor's bills 'of the friendly Herr Dr Freund . . . This Jew demands so much, because he himself stands at the brink of bankruptcy',[33] Marx informed Engels. Jenny and Lenchen tried to pay off the most pressing bills by making visits to pawnshops. Karl fled into the British Museum and reflected about the coming revolutions that would also change his life fundamentally.

As chance would have it, a Sunday Law passed by Parliament, prohibiting the printing of newspapers and the opening of places of entertainment, restaurants and pubs, was met with violent opposition. The Chartists declared that the law was directed against the workers, because the rich could amuse themselves in their clubs on Sundays as well as on any other day. They called a mass demonstration in Hyde Park to show the ladies and gentlemen who were riding there what the people thought of such a law. There were some incidents, but nothing overtly revolutionary, although Marx announced categorically in an article he wrote the following day for the *Neue Oder Zeitung*: 'Yesterday the English Revolution began in Hyde Park.'[34]

In the midst of this refugee misery came the unexpected news of 'a very happy event. Yesterday we learned of the death of my wife's 90-year-old uncle',[35] wrote Marx to Engels. Jenny would inherit £100 or more 'unless the old dog leaves part of his fortune to his housekeeper'.[36] Jenny herself told a friend that she had inherited a small sum of about £150–£200 from an old relative in Scotland, for

> my grandmother, the mother of my late, dear father, was a Scotchwoman by birth, from one of the first Scottish families, the family Campbell & Argyle. The Duke of Argyle is thus a close relation of these ancestors, and when I married, my darling mother gave me much magnificent silverware that came from Scotland bearing the Argyle coat of arms. Silver and coats of arms have, of course, long since slipped 'from the blue bed to the brown' as a result of our expulsions, migrations and emigrations, and the little bit I have been able to save from the shipwreck is mostly in the hands of 'uncle'.[37]

It cannot be proved whether Jenny actually received a Scottish inheritance, or whether she wrote these lines to impress on the friend that she came from a very good family (just as she indicated on her visiting card that she was born a baroness – a fact, incidentally, that occasionally caused embarrassment to the prophet of the dictatorship of the proletariat and made him exclaim: 'Beware of your baroness cards!'[38]), but the prospect of being temporarily liberated from her wretched financial worries by an inheritance made it possible for Jenny to realize a long-entertained hope – to visit her old mother and her hometown of Trier. She felt guilty that she could not ease the last years of her beloved mother's life and that the news she sent from London to Trier was not very encouraging. She had told her mother by letter of the deaths of her three children and Caroline, who had lost a child herself, knew how grievously her daughter was suffering, and longed to console her in person. But how could Jenny, the wife of the communist leader expelled from Prussia, obtain a passport for a journey to Trier? However, Jenny solved that question herself by appealing to her half-brother Ferdinand and asking him to help her get a passport. Ferdinand saw to it immediately, just as he always tried to help his 'prodigal sister'. In April 1856, Marx informed Engels that 'my wife has received a passport on his Majesty's special order. She is going to Trier with the whole family for 3 to 4 months.'[39] Jenny left London with her three children worrying about her husband, who had been ill the whole week complaining of severe rheumatism in his back.

The sight of her eighty-year-old mother shocked Jenny, for Caroline von Westphalen was partially paralysed and had to rely on the help of strangers. But the unexpected reunion with her daughter gave her new vitality. She was charmed by her three grandchildren, whom she had never seen before: the twelve-year-old Jenny, eleven-year-old Laura, and the cheerful baby Eleanor. Politics were not discussed. Caroline chose not to consider Karl as the chief of the communist conspiracy, as the reactionary German press did, but as the foreign correspondent of the largest American newspaper. She shared Jenny's joy when Jenny read her some paragraphs from a wonderful love letter she received at the end of June from Karl. He had gone to Engels in Manchester, because he said he needed a change of air, but probably also because he wanted to escape from the eternally threatening creditors of Dean Street. Now he was sitting alone in a room in Manchester and before him lay a picture of the woman he had married fourteen years ago.

> Dearest heart, no matter how bad your picture is, it is a very great help to me and I understand now, how even the 'black Madonnas', the most disgraceful portraits of the Mother of God, could find undying admirers, even more admirers than the good portraits. In any case, none of any of these black madonna pictures has ever been more loved, looked at and adored than your photograph. I have you right here, in front of me and carry you in my hands, kissing you from head to foot and sigh, kneeling in front of you: 'Madam, I love you'.[40]

Jenny smiled when she read these last words from the familiar Heine poem. But then there were passages in this long love letter that moved her to tears:

The moment you are away from me, my love for you appears for what it is, a giant that contains all the energy of my mind and all the character of my heart. I feel again that I am a man, because I feel a great passion, and the diversity that studies and modern education give us, and the scepticism with which we necessarily criticize all subjective and objective impressions, can easily make us all small and weak and cross. But my love, not for Feuerbach's man, not for Moleschott's metabolism, not for the proletariat, but my love for the loved one and particularly for you, makes the man again a man.[41]

When Jenny read these words she would have liked to rush to Manchester at once to prove to her beloved husband that she too still had the same feelings for him that she had had fourteen years ago – in spite of everything. But Caroline's 81st birthday was on 11 July and Jenny wanted to celebrate it with her because she knew that it was probably the last time she could be with her beloved mother on that day. In fact, Caroline died twelve days after her birthday. Once again, as so often in Jenny's life, there was a sudden change from joy to sadness.

She was the only relative at her mother's grave and had to take care of the estate, which meant entering into negotiations with her half-brother Ferdinand in Berlin. She was pleased that he answered at once and very cordially, too. He called her 'my dear cherished Jenny'[42] and lamented the death of 'our dear honoured mother . . . what an irreparable loss for you and all of us'.[43] Concerning Caroline's estate, there was no question in Ferdinand's mind 'that you and Edgar are the heirs'.[44] In case there were debts, or 'if you need money at the moment, please write me and I shall send it at once'.[45] Such words were balm to Jenny's ears. If Ferdinand only knew what financial difficulties she had had to cope with in her life! She informed Karl at once that she could dispose of her mother's estate and Karl wrote Engels: 'I received a letter from my wife today. She seems much affected by the death of the old woman. She will spend eight to ten days in Trier to auction off the insignificant personal effects of the old woman and share the proceeds with Edgar.'[46]

The dissolution of her mother's household was a very sad affair for Jenny, because with it she lost her last ties to her homeland. The thought that she would soon have to live in Dean Street again made her sick. She wrote to her husband that, before coming to London with the children, she would travel to Jersey and spend September and October there resting from the strains of her German experience. Karl wrote 'the plan is excellent',[47] but he did not know how to finance it. He was destitute once again because the *New York Daily Tribune* had rejected some of his articles.

In the end he and Jenny decided to leave the Street of Death as soon as the inherited money arrived and to move 'with a joyful heart into a small house at the foot of the romantic Hampstead Heath, not far from the charming Primrose Hill'.[48] 'When we slept for the first time in our own beds, sat on our own chairs and even had a parlour with second-hand furniture in rococo style, or rather "bric-à-brac", we really believed we lived in a magic castle and we payed homage to our young magnificence with drums and trumpets.'[49]

10

At the Edge of the Abyss

I

Jenny's magic castle was a small house, built in a typical middle-class English terrace style, in a new development on the edge of Hampstead Heath, a popular place for excursions of London's city dwellers. The Marx family also enjoyed a Sunday on Hampstead Heath. It was a walk of about an hour and a half from Dean Street and, according to Liebknecht, undertaken in the following order: 'I was on the vanguard with the two girls, either telling stories or playing games . . . Then came the main force of the army: Marx with his wife and some Sunday visitor, who required a certain attention. And behind them Lenchen with the hungriest of the guests, who helped her carrying the picnic hamper.'[1] It was a blessing to be able to spend a few hours in the open air after the oppressive closeness of their Soho flat. In the autumn of 1856 she could report: 'After long and strenuous journeys of exploration, we have finally found a particularly nice house. It lies in the most beautiful and healthiest part of London, not far from Hampstead Heath, which you probably know by name and which is famous for its beautiful situation and the purity of its air.'[2] Thus Jenny described her new home five days after they moved into it going on to relate how it is surrounded by fresh, green meadows on which sheep, horses, goats and chickens were romping around; 'in the distance the colossal, gigantic town of London can be seen in dim outline. In the basement of the house there is a kitchen, laundry room and a so-called breakfast room; the garden next to it is somewhat small, but big enough for a large hen house . . . On the first floor are two parlours, on the second, one fair sized room, a bedroom and also a small cloak room, on the third floor the same distribution of rooms. And then there is still a spacious attic storeroom for suitcases and boxes.'[3]

Compared with the dreary attic flat in which they had to live for seven years, the little house at 9 Grafton Terrace, Maitland Park, Haverstock Hill, was indeed a magic castle. According to English custom, it was covered with carpets 'from top to bottom'. 'The children are very happy in the many new rooms, and little Eleanor, captivated with delight, is kissing the "nice carpets" and the little dog who is lying on the felt hearth-rug.'[4]

After fourteen years of marriage they now entered on the path of respectability. '*La vie de Bohème* had come to an end and instead of openly carrying on the struggle against poverty in exile, we now had to maintain at least the *appearance* of respectability. We were sailing with all sails set into bourgeois life. And yet there were still the same petty pressures, the same struggles, the same old misery, the same intimate relationship with the three balls of the pawnshop – what was gone was the humour . . .'[5]

Not only the humour: Jenny's health was gone, too. Shortly after moving into her new home she went to bed and was ill for months. Her physician, Dr Allen, assumed that it was a nervous disease and prescribed all kinds of medicines. Jenny herself suspected that the reason for her sickness was an unwanted pregnancy, for it became obvious to her around the turn of the year 1856–7 that she would have her seventh child in the summer. The thought made her physically ill: none of her six confinements had been easy, suckling was so painful that she had to give it up, and a wet-nurse had to be employed which cost money. Her small inheritance was soon used up and the Dean Street spectre of poverty came to lurk in Hampstead where the necessity of maintaining the appearance of prosperity had to be maintained, particularly because the girls were now getting a high school education in the South Hampstead College for Ladies. The two older ones knew that it was often hard for their father to provide £8 for school fees, but they did not show their school friends what life was like at home. Jennychen and Laura were industrious, learned easily, and frequently won prizes. Jenny was proud of them and wished she could satisfy their little material wishes; but that was beyond her financial resources, because Karl lost half his income in 1857 as a result of the American economic crisis. To be sure, Dana proposed that he collaborate on *The New American Cyclopedia*, which was being published by a group of American journalists, but this did not last long. Hence, as before, the family had to rely on occasional royalties, on financial support from Engels and on future inheritances. But while they formerly shared their financial worries with the other refugees in Soho, they were now completely alone. 'It took a long time before I got used to this complete seclusion. I often longed for my extensive walks through the busy streets of the West End, to my meetings, our clubs and the familiar pub with its cozy chitchat, where I had often forgotten for a time the worries of life'.[6]

Marx also found it hard to get used to the rural environment of his little house. He was a city animal and loved the long political discussions with young party members in Windmill Street or in the pubs of Tottenham Court Road. This was not as easy as before because of their distance from Hampstead; the trip to the British Museum also took much longer than it had from Dean Street. 'Besides', wrote Jenny, 'our pretty little house was almost inaccessible. No smooth road led to us, there was construction everywhere, you had to work your way through heaps of rubble, and in rainy weather the heavy clay mud stuck so thickly to the soles of your feet that you got home worn out from the struggle . . . rather than venturing out at night into darkness, mud and heaps of rock, you preferred sitting in front of the warm open fire.'[7]

The monotony of her life in the months before her confinement with her seventh child was relieved by the appearance of a new young person into the family. Marianne Kreutz, Lenchen's half-sister, came to London in April from St Wendel. She was 22 years old, a kind girl, and a hard worker. Together with Lenchen she kept the house for five years, so Jenny was able to devote herself entirely to her husband's projects. He was making preparations for his major opus in spite of his time-consuming mission of obtaining the necessary means for their daily bread through loans or promissory notes. He called it the *Critique of Political Economy*, but he could not work on it as much as he wished because he, too, fell ill again with his old liver complaint and was stuffed with drugs and pills.

Such was their condition, when on 6 July Jenny gave birth to a girl. Marx informed Engels that 'the child . . . died at once. This is no misfortune in itself. However, the circumstances that brought it about are such that reminiscence is agonizing'.[8] Engels was shocked by this news 'in spite of the mystery. You can accept the death of the child stoically. But your wife cannot.'[9] Jenny, indeed, stayed in bed for weeks, and even when she felt physically better, Marx observed: 'She is still in bed and extremely upset; I do not blame her for that *au fond de coeur*, under present auspices, although it annoys me.'[10]

What Marx called 'upset' was a deep melancholy. The thought of her four dead children haunted her and it is doubtful whether she would have had the strength to go on living but for her three girls – two of whom were later to take their own lives. Marx, too, had moments when 'he preferred to lie 100 feet under the earth than to continue vegetating'.[11] How desperate his economic situation was is described in his letters to Engels imploring for help. The latter was earning so much in his father's firm that he could keep a horse, ride to the hounds and join exclusive clubs. Marx told him:

Even if I were to cut back our expenses to the bone – i.e. take the girls from their school, move into a proletarian house, dismiss the maids, live on potatoes – the auction of all our furniture would not bring in enough money to pay all the creditors around us and assure an unhindered retreat into some kind of hole. The only means of preventing a collapse is the show of respectability we been able to maintain. I, myself, could not care less if we lived in Whitechapel, if only I got an hour's rest and could continue my work. But such a metamorphosis could have dangerous consequences for my wife in her present condition and it would hardly be suitable for the growing girls. [12]

Engels answered as always by return mail. He sent his 'dear Moor' £40 with the advice: 'It is about time you approached your old woman again or some Dutchman.' [13] He adopted the expression 'old woman' from Marx, who always called his mother that, and the 'Dutchmen' were the well-to-do relatives that Jenny had once visited and asked for help. Engels concludes his letter thus: 'In any case, let us burn this correspondence so that the whole matter stays between us.' [14] Marx did not follow the advice of his friend in this case, but there is no doubt that many documents of the Marx family have been burned, especially those relating to the private lives of Jenny and Karl.

After receiving Engels' money, Marx sent his suffering wife, who was badly in need of rest, for a four-week vacation to Ramsgate, a popular seaside resort in Kent. She was alone for the first few days and made the acquaintance of Anna Bella Carlisle, who had just published two novels. Miss Carlisle was the sister of Mrs Cunningham, whose two daughters were friends of the Marx girls. Jenny reports that Mrs Cunningham too was an author and was working at several English and Scottish family histories. It has been assumed, but so far without proof, that Jenny, who also enjoyed writing, was also trying to write novels at this time.

Her four weeks' stay in Ramsgate was a pleasant interlude in her 'monotonous still-life' in London. Lenchen brought the three girls down and they spent two wonderful weeks together. She was alone again for the last week and when she returned home 'tanned like a mulatto by the sharp sea air, she was received with great rejoicing in the prettily decorated house.'[15]

But the joy did not last long. Housekeeping money became scarce again and the demands of bakers, butchers and green-grocers had to be fielded. But since – thanks to Lassalle's good offices – a German publisher was willing to publish the first volume of Marx's fifteen years of researches into the history and workings of capitalism, there were hopes of income from royalties. The manuscript had to be written up, of course, then copied into legible hand by Jenny and that always took longer than planned. 'Here at home it looks more dreary and desolate than ever',[16] Marx wrote to Engels in English in December. 'Since my wife cannot make Christmas preparations for the children herself, but is bothered instead with unpaid bills from all sides, has to copy my manuscript and in between run downtown to the pawnshops, the mood is extremely gloomy'.[17] Engels' answer was £5 and a Christmas basket, filled with bottles of port, sherry and champagne.

When the 'ill-fated manuscript'[18] was finally ready in January 1859, it could not be sent to the German publisher Duncker in Berlin, since Marx did not even have enough money for the postage. Engels took care of this too, but it took months before Duncker printed the book, because he first wanted to publish Lassalle's play *Franz von Sickingen*. 'That swine Duncker is happy that he now has another excuse for postponing payment of my royalties. I shall never forget this trick of the little Jew [Lassalle],'[19] wrote Marx to Engels in May 1859. One month later Marx's *Critique of Political Economy*, Part I, finally appeared in an edition of a thousand copies.

But Jenny's high hopes for Karl's book were not fulfilled, as she admitted in December, for it was hardly noted by the German press. Detailed investigations of goods and their use and exchange value were neither interesting nor comprehensible to the general public, and the number of trained economists was too small to gain readers for the book by reviewing it, although Engels and other friends of the Marx Party living in England tried to place reviews in German papers.

II

While Jenny had to struggle continuously against her financial miseries, which 'have never been so wretched as now, when our sweet, gracefully growing girls have to suffer them also',[20] Karl became embroiled in a grotesque libel action, which kept him from doing any other work for months. It started with a pamphlet entitled 'Warning' which appeared on 18 June in *Das Volk*, a small German newspaper in London, for which Marx wrote occasional articles, and which was reproduced in the Augsburg *Allgemeine Zeitung* on 22 June. The warning was directed against the well-known German naturalist Carl Vogt, who was trying to gain collaborators for a German newspaper he had founded in Switzerland. Its purpose was to make propaganda on behalf of Napoleon III and against Austria, because he believed that the existence of Austria prevented the union of Germany. Marx's pamphlet claimed that Vogt was a paid French agent.

Vogt, who considered this assertion a defamation, brought a suit against the editors of the *Allgemeine Zeitung* at the district court of Augsburg. After a lengthy hearing, the district court rejected the suit on the grounds that it belonged to the Court of Assizes. Thereupon Vogt published a 200-page pamphlet entitled *My Suit Against the 'Allgemeine Zeitung'*. It contained extensive descriptions by his lawyer of the activities of the 'gang of rowdies', a secret communist conspiracy of German refugees in London, who under the leadership of Karl Marx proclaimed the dictatorship of the proletariat, but in reality were blackmailing their members in Germany into sending protection money, threatening denunciation to the police.

Marx was beside himself with rage when he heard, 'what blackguardly, foul remarks against me'[21] Vogt's pamphlet contained. He declared it not only defiled his reputation, but brought the party into disrepute with the German workers. He had to defend himself against this even though old friends of the party like Freiligrath advised him to let the matter drop. Engels, too, was of that opinion at first and was only ready to denounce Vogt's lies, when Marx told him that 'Vogt, that swine, is trying to fool the German philistines into believing that I am living here at the expense of the workers'[22] (no one knew better than Engels that this was a lie). He could not understand why Marx told him 'I am of course not telling my wife anything of this shit',[23] nor had Engels understood a remark that Jenny had made recently in a letter to him 'without Karl's knowledge I have turned to him (Ferdinand) for money'.[24] Why should two people have secrets from each other who were living in an obviously happy marriage?

If Marx really thought he could keep Vogt's accusations secret from Jenny, he deceived himself. She took an active interest in all his work, not only because she believed in his ideas but because the existence of her family depended on the royalties he received. She worried when she watched him trying for months to refute Vogt's smears, instead of writing articles for the *Tribune*. 'The Moor asks you to concoct an article, if at all possible by Friday or Saturday',[25] she wrote to Engels in August 1860, 'Several have unfortunately not been written'.[26] This was not the only such occasion. For in 1860 Marx had only one aim: to destroy Karl Vogt, the enemy of his party, in print as well as legally. In February he started an action for defamation against the *Berliner Nationalzeitung* after it reprinted portions of Vogt's 'nothing-but-shit book',[27] thus opening itself up to legal attack. The lawsuit went through four stages but was quashed before a public hearing could be held. Hence it was even more important to annihilate Vogt in print. Marx dedicated himself to this, despite his worsening 'horrible liver troubles'[28] and his constant shortage of funds.

Jenny, who helped him by copying the manuscript, urged him to finish it, because she did not expect much money from an anti-Vogt pamphlet. The main reason it was taking so long was Marx's attempt to analyse and refute a long letter by the Prussian ex-lieutenant von Techow quoted in Vogt's pamphlet. Techow writes that in August 1850 he had visited the leader of the Communist League, Karl Marx, in London and had spent an evening in a pub with him, Engels and a few other members of the League:

> First we drank port, then claret, i.e. red Bordeaux, then champagne. Marx was completely drunk after the red wine. That was exactly what I wanted, for he became more candid than he would have been otherwise. I ascertained many things that I might only have suspected. In spite of his condition, Marx was in complete control of the conversation up to the end. He gave the impression not only of rare mental superiority but of an important personality. I would go through fire for him, if he had as much heart as mind, as much love as hate . . . I regret, for the sake of our common goal, that this man does not have a noble heart in addition to his eminent mind. But I am convinced that the most dangerous personal ambition has eaten up everything good in him. He makes fun of the fools that believe his proletarian catechism, just as he does of the communists *à la* Willich and of the bourgeois. The only people he respects are the aristocrats, the real ones, aristocrats from conviction. He says he needs a force to drive them from power and has found that force only in the proletarians, which is why he is basing his system on them. In spite of all his assurances to the contrary, and perhaps because of them, I have the impression that the purpose of all his activities is to attain personal power.[29]

It is understandable that Marx was stung by such a portrait of himself written by a hopeful disciple of his party. Jenny too must have been annoyed that Karl could make such an impression, even though she may have admitted to herself that Karl was partly responsible.

While she was copying the pamphlet that Karl at first wanted to call *Da Da Vogt* in a sarcastic allusion to an Arab called Da Da who had written a eulogy of Napoleon III, she wrote to Engels that the whole thing was being dragged out because Karl was being far too thorough: 'I simply cannot stand the analysis of the Techow letter; there seems to be a snag . . . Unfortunately no steps have been taken to find a publisher'.[30] It soon became obvious that it was impossible to find a German publisher for *Herr Vogt*. Marx had it printed in London at his own expense, at a cost of £25, a sum his family could have lived on for several months. His hopes that he might recoup his investment by sales of the pamphlet turned out to be illusory. The bomb – as he called the pamphlet that he threw into the German party landscape – proved to be a dud. 'The deliberate silence of the press', writes Jenny, 'was of course responsible for the sale of the book not being as good as we had every right to expect'.[31] Only Karl's closest friends found the sarcastic wit of the pamphlet exciting and considered it an important chapter in the history of their time.

Jenny fell ill shortly after she had copied the manuscript and handed it over to the printer. 'I was seized by the most terrible fever and the doctor had to be called in. He came on 20 November, examined me carefully for a long time and said after a long silence: "My dear Mrs Marx, I am sorry to say you have smallpox – the children must leave the house immediately".'[32] The following days and weeks were terrible. The children were sent to the Liebknechts', who lived nearby, and Karl and Lenchen, who had been vaccinated, took care of the gravely ill Jenny. Her fever shot so high that she had to put ice on her lips and from time to time Bordeaux wine. She could hardly swallow and was losing her hearing rapidly: 'Finally my eyes closed and I did not know whether they would remain forever in eternal darkness.'[33]

Even after the crisis had passed she was shocked to see her disfigured face in the mirror. 'I looked like a rhinoceros that belonged in the zoo rather than a member of the Caucasian race'.[34] The girls wept when they saw their mother whom they had left five weeks ago as a good-looking woman. It was months before she again looked like a human being.

Two events occurred at this time that were of great importance to the Marx family. On the accession to the throne of King William I of Prussia in January 1861, an amnesty was declared for all political emigrants permitting them an un-hindered return home. The second event was the election of Lincoln to the presidency of the United States and the be-ginning of the conflict between the northern and southern states. This conflict, which grew into the Civil War, caused the editorial department of the *New York Daily Tribune* to give notice to all its foreign correspondents; the American people, who were now completely absorbed in their own affairs, were no longer interested in events abroad. As a result of this decision, Marx lost his only regular source of income.

When the burden of debts had again risen so high, as a consequence of Jenny's illness and Karl's liver complaints, that the bailiff appeared, 'Karl decided to undertake a raid to Holland, to the country of his forefathers, of tobacco and cheese. He wants to see if he can wheedle a few coins out of his uncle. If he succeeds, he will make a secret trip to Berlin to see about starting a monthly or weekly paper, for our recent experiences have convinced us that without our own organ we cannot exist.'[35]

Marx left London at the end of February 1861 with a passport made out to a Mr Buhring. He informed Engels before he left that he had had a lot of trouble getting the money together for the journey. He had been forced to ask some of his creditors for deferred payments with the explanation that the American crisis had affected his major source of income. They had agreed 'however only on condition that my wife would pay *weekly* during my absence',[36] which meant that Engels had to send Jenny money for her household every week.

From her husband she heard nothing for a long time. He spent a few pleasant weeks in the house of his well-to-do uncle, Lion Philips, in the Dutch town of Zaltbommel, where he flirted with his young and charming cousin Nannette before travelling on to Berlin. There he was enthusiastically received by his admirer Lassalle, who introduced him as the leading theoretician of socialism. Lassalle lived in a beautiful house in one of the most affluent parts of Berlin and was supported so generously by his patroness, Countess Hatzfeldt, that he had no financial worries. He proposed that Marx, and perhaps some of the other former collaborators on the *Neue Rheinische Zeitung*, should come to Berlin and establish a newspaper. He would contribute some 20 to 30 thousand thalers, on condition that he too would be an editor-in-chief. The idea of once again becoming the editor of a German newspaper was very tempting for Marx; what disturbed him was Lassalle's demand that he be an equal partner in the enterprise. But since he had to find a way out of his present situation for purely economic reasons, he discussed the plan in detail. The first step was to apply for the restoration of his Prussian citizenship which he had given up years ago, for he could not remain in Berlin as a stateless person. While he was awaiting a decision, Lassalle and the Countess introduced him to Berlin society. 'To insult the royal family, Countess Hatzfeldt took me to an opera box right next to that of handsome William and accomplices',[37] he wrote to Engels. And to his 'cruel little witch' Nannette he wrote: 'On Thursday Lassalle gave a dinner in honour of my return, to which he invited a number of ladies and gentlemen. Among the more famous ones were old General von Pfuel, the painter of battle scenes, Bleibtreu, Privy Councillor Förster [a well-known Prussian historian] and so on. Privy Councillor Förster proposed a toast to little me.'[38]

The irony with which the prophet of the red spectre describes this toast in Berlin to his sweet Dutch cousin is admirable; it was less admirable that for a long time he did not write anything to Jenny about where he was or what he was doing. He sent her 50 thalers at the end of March but gave her no further news. In a letter Jenny wrote to Nannette, she mentions that her girls were shocked 'when they learned from German papers that their venerable papa was planning to move to Berlin with his family'.[39] And when she heard from Lassalle how pleased people were with the return of the prodigal son, she answered: 'You are holding out great hopes to me for an early return to the fatherland. But honestly, I have quite lost the fatherland, dear fatherland. I have looked for it in the smallest and remotest corners of my heart and have found no fatherland. Conditions in our "dear faithful Germany", this *mater dolorosa* of poets, are so unpleasant that they disgust more than attract.'[40] She added that it would be very hard for her to return to Germany just now anyway, because her face had become so ugly and pockmarked.

Marx, on the other hand, assured Lassalle that 'he would move to Berlin for a half-year or so',[41] if his petition for repatriation was approved. To his uncle Philips he wrote: 'My wife is against a move to Berlin, mainly because she does not want our daughters being introduced into the Hatzfeldt circle.'[42]

In the end, the question of the Marxes' return to Germany was decided by the Royal Prussian Chief of Police von Zedlitz, who rejected Marx's application for repatriation. Before Marx returned to London, he paid a brief visit to his old mother in Trier, who cancelled some of his debt certificates, and travelled once again to Zaltbommel, where his entire time was taken up 'by talks with my uncle, on the one hand, and on the other by courting my cousin.'[43] Having been away for more than four months he returned to London at the end of 1861, loaded with presents.

Jenny wrote Lassalle: 'There was rejoicing, when suddenly and unexpectedly the Moor arrived last Monday. We talked till late at night, looked at things he brought, laughed, hugged and kissed. I am particularly happy to be relieved of my temporary reins of rule and to again feel that I am a "subject".'[44]

'The leaking ship of state was set afloat again with the Dutch money and for a time we sailed on cheerfully.'[45] A few days after Karl's return, a Dutch cousin, Nannette's brother Jacques, announced that he was coming to London. Hence the little house 'had to be quickly trimmed for the solemn reception of our guest, and the worthy married couple had to withdraw to the upper regions of the house in order to give the stranger the so-called state bedroom (rococo style *c'est à dire* bric-à-brac)'.[46] The visit coincided with Jennychen's 17th birthday on 1 May – 'our sweet, dark-eyed Jennychen'.[47] And it was a real joy! 'There was cooking and baking, dancing, singing and fun!'[48]

III

As usual the joy was short-lived, for the Dutch money was soon spent and Jennychen's health deteriorated visibly. She was suffering from an obstinate cough that emaciated her and worried her parents greatly for several years. Tussy too, who had just started school, became ill. She suffered from a kind of jaundice, a disease that mostly affected adults. Jenny tried in vain to get some household money by selling some of her husband's books. And, as always, Marx turned to Engels for help. 'My wife tells me every day she wished she were in the grave with her children, and I cannot really blame her for it, for the humiliations, vexations and torments which she has to suffer, are indeed indescribable'.[49]

While Jenny tried to keep her family going by repeated trips to the pawnshop, Marx worked desperately on his book on the history of capitalism and its inevitable collapse. 'I am expanding this volume', he wrote to Engels, 'because the German dogs judge the value of books by their cubic contents'.[50] But his hopes of obtaining an advance from a German publisher remained unfulfilled. This was the situation when Lassalle wrote, saying he would be coming to London for a few weeks in July on the occasion of the 1862 Exhibition. Jenny was horrified when she heard this and on the last pages of her autobiographical notes she describes how revolted she was by Lassalle's theatrical posturing and claims of genius. She was very angry that he 'wanted to become the messiah of the German workers'[51] and that he espoused her husband's idea without understanding them. Marx, who tried to get a loan from Lassalle, was also glad when 'the Jewish Nigger'[52] left again, for 'the fellow would rather throw his money into the dirt than lend it to a friend . . . He assumes he has to live like a Jewish baron, or like a Jew raised to the rank of a baron (probably by the Countess). Imagine, this fellow, who knows what's going on in America, hence knows the crisis in which I find myself, had the audacity to ask me if I would entrust one of my daughters to Countess Hatzfeldt as her "lady companion" . . . and since I didn't have any business to take care of right now but was merely doing some theoretical work, I might just as well kill my time with him.'[53]

It may seem surprising that, despite these bitter lines, Marx informed Lassalle, before the latter's departure in August 1862, of his precarious financial situation as a result of the loss of his American income and that Lassalle was willing to sign a promissory note for 400 thalers. Thus, catastrophe was averted once again, the bailiff left and Jenny could go to the seaside at Ramsgate for some weeks with the children. This was particularly important for Jennychen, whose health was very poor. Marx called her 'the most excellent and gifted child in the world. But she is suffering here for two reasons: first, because of her health and secondly, because of our bourgeois troubles.'[54]

While his family was trying to forget their London difficulties at Ramsgate, Marx travelled to his Dutch relations and once again to his mother in Trier. But he failed to get another advance on his paternal inheritance. His old mother told him only that he should finally get another job because he obviously could not make a living as a journalist. Uncle Lion Philips, too, who had always helped him, suggested he apply for a position at the London railway office that he would procure for him. Marx wrote to a surprised Engels that he was considering entering a railway office: however, his bad handwriting prevented him from getting the position!

By the end of the year things were so bad, despite Engels' help, that Marx decided to send his wife to Paris to approach a rich French friend for support. In her autobiographical notes Jenny relates what happened there:

I arrived at the good friend's home in bitter cold and sick with worries, only to find that he had suffered a stroke and was hardly recognizable. He died a few days after my coming. I returned home desperate and immediately on entering our house heard the terrible and painful news that a few hours before my arrival our good, dear, faithful Marianne, Lenchen's sister, had passed away from a heart illness, gently and blessedly like a big child. The good, faithful, hard-working girl had been with us for five years. I loved her and was so much attached to her that her loss hurt me deeply. I lost a loyal, devoted, friendly creature whom I shall never forget. She was conducted to her place of eternal rest on the second day of Christmas.[55]

In a letter to Engels of 24 December 1862, Marx describes Jenny's journey to France, which was pursued by misfortune from beginning to end. It started with a terrible storm on the channel, then a train delay, then the overturn of an omnibus and finally, when she arrived in London, 'the cab in which she was sitting was run into by another'.[56] But what was even worse, he had to pay the undertaker £7 10*s.* for Marianne's funeral – 'a nice Christmas spectacle for the poor children.'[57]

The simple comforts of the family were threatened with collapse more than once in the weeks that followed. The winter was cold and because there was no money for coal, they either froze or stayed in bed to keep warm. The girls could not go to school because their tuition had not been paid for the past term and also because they had no shoes. To have at least some money for food Jenny turned, behind Karl's back, to their old friend Lupus, who got along as well as he could by giving private lessons in Manchester. He sent her £2 by return mail. At almost the same time Engels informed them that Mary Burns, his mistress for twenty years, had died of a heart attack. 'I cannot tell you what I feel like. The poor girl has loved me with her whole heart.'[58]

As his answer to this news, Marx wrote only that Mary's death surprised and dismayed him and then he entered into a lengthy digression about his own financial worries. From Jenny no line of sympathy. She had never approved of Engels' 'living in sin' with this Irish textile worker. If Jenny had been wise, she would have given the appearance of sympathy by writing a few words. As it was, Engels was deeply hurt by the indifference of his friend and Jenny, 'for all my friends, including mere philistine acquaintances, have shown me more sympathy and friendship on this occasion which distressed me grievously.'[59]

By way of apology, Marx wrote to Engels that the news of Mary's death had reached them at a time when the bailiff was in the house, a butcher was pestering for payment of a bill, when they had neither coal nor food and Jennychen was ill in bed. 'What really made me angry was the fact that my wife thought I had never given you a true picture of our real situation'.[60] But he had finally brought his wife to accept the following proposal: 'I shall write to all my creditors that I will declare myself bankrupt by filing a bill in the court of bankruptcy, if they don't stop bothering me . . . My two oldest children will get positions as governesses . . . Lenchen will take up another position, and I will move with my wife and Tussychen into the same City Model Lodging where the red Wolff once lived with his family.'[61]

Engels was horrified at this, for he considered a declaration of bankruptcy by the leader of the communist world movement unthinkable, even though he was upset with Marx. Since he did not have any large amount of cash available at the moment, 'he dared making a very risky deal'[62] by signing over to Marx a bankable bill of £100 made out to a customer of the firm Ermen and Engels. In addition, Jenny received some money from a rich Jewish lady in Germany, who had heard how badly off the family was. Once again they were safe for a while and Marx could continue his researches in the British Museum. In addition to his studies, he watched the political events in America and on the Continent with great interest. He was particularly impressed by the revolutionary uprising of the Polish people against their Russian oppressors. 'What do you think about this Polish affair?'[63] he asked Engels. 'This much is certain, the era of revolution is fairly open again in

Europe'.[64] Engels, too, thought that the Poles were 'really tremendous fellows'[65] and believed that revolution was also standing at Russia's door. They both considered publishing a manifesto to spread the idea in Germany that the re-establishment of a Polish nation was in the Germans' interest. But nothing came of it because Marx was temporarily prevented from writing by an eye infection.

However, it was not only his eyes that made working difficult. He was alarmed when painful boils appeared all over his body, and illness was indeed a constant guest in the family: 'My wife has been confined to bed for two weeks and is almost deaf, God knows why. Jennychen again has a kind of diphtheria attack. It would be very kind if you could send some wine for both of them (Dr Allen says it should be port for Jennychen)'.[66]

And then something happened that was particularly detrimental to the health of Karl and Jenny: On 23 May 1863 Ferdinand Lassalle was elected President of the General German Workers' Union, the first independent organization of German workers. Engels considered it a scandal that Lassalle had been elected and not Marx. He admonished his friend to finish his book 'so that we have something substantial to talk about'.[67] Jenny, too, felt that 'the ill-fated book is weighing on all of us like a nightmare. If only the leviathan were launched.'[68] But that could not be done for the time being, for the furunculous boils that had afflicted Karl for years turned into large, bloody boils, carbuncles, which had to be removed surgically. In the presence of Jenny and Lenchen, who had to wash off streaming, purulent blood, Dr Allen cut a carbuncle as large as a fist out of Marx's back, without taking the time to get pain-relieving drugs, because he considered the disease life-threatening.

Jenny reports that Karl's serious illness lasted four weeks. During this period she lay at night on the floor next to her husband's bed, comforted him and gave him wine that Engels had sent. Since there was again no housekeeping money, she sent Lenchen to the pawnshop with some silver spoons. She writes in her memoirs that there were, in addition to the physical sufferings, 'gnawing worries, mental tortures of all kinds. We were standing almost at the edge of the abyss, when we suddenly received the news of my mother-in-law's death'.[69] Only by this event did Marx finally come into possession of his father's inheritance. But it was necessary to travel to Trier to take care of the estate, 'even though he had one foot in the grave'.[70]

Dr Allen not only gave his permission for the journey, he believed that a change of air might be good for his patient. Since Marx needed money for travelling, he wrote to Engels on 2 December 1863: 'Two hours ago a telegram arrived saying that my mother was dead. Fate demands that one of us be home . . . I must ask you to send me enough money *by return mail* so that I can start the journey to Trier *immediately*'.[71] On the next day Engels sent him £10 and on 7 December Marx left his family with the wound in his back still unhealed. He hoped to be back before Christmas with his paternal inheritance.

But that is not what happened. After trying in vain for two weeks to unseal the papers and bonds left by his mother in Trier, he went to his Dutch relatives and wrote to Engels that it would take four to six weeks before he got his money. 'But since my wife has to pay a butcher's bill of £10 (i.e. a note) on 10 January 1864, I would be grateful if you could take care of it'.[72] His body took revenge on him during this time of waiting by forming another 'cursed carbuncle' on exactly the same spot as the old one. But he was well taken care of by his old uncle Lion Philips and his 'witty cousin with her dangerous black eyes',[73] while his family back in London spent a lonely Christmas.

After the turn of the year Jenny wrote her 'darling Karl' a long letter, wondering why she had not heard from him:

I am afraid you are frozen up or snowed in in the Lazy Land (Freiligrath's expression); here it is freezing lumps of ice and you need mountains of coal to make our tiny rooms comfortable. If I did not know that you are in the blessed land, I would feel very, very much deserted now at this Christmas time, when home and family are the watchwords of the day. It was a relief to know that in your illness you are being looked after with loving care and this thought helped me to get over many things . . .

I had hoped until now to get a bulletin from you, but since it seems that I am again drawing a blank, I am seizing this '*couleur de rose initiative*' to put an end to eight days without correspondence. If I only knew that you are quite well again! . . . The little one can scarcely wait for you to return and says daily, my dada is coming today. She enjoys her holidays thoroughly and since she did not have a Christmas tree, her sisters made her more than 20 dolls in all sorts of costumes. Among the grotesque figures one fencer is Ruy Blas and an excellent Chinaman with a long train which the children made from Tussy's hair and glued on to the bald Kui Kui . . .

Once we took the whole gang to the theatre to watch the famous American actress Miss Bateman, in the role of Judie Lea. That was a delight . . . and we came home in a cab very happily . . . The children are still tired from last night and don't want to do any writing. They are sending hearty greetings to you and those around you, and so do I. Now goodbye old boy! Let me hear from you soon.[74]

In her memoirs Jenny wrote only: 'It was a terrible time – a lonely, miserable winter!'[75]

11

Politics as Fate

I

Jenny's only consolation during this lonely, dismal winter was the presence of her three vivacious daughters. She thought that all three were very attractive, even though she realized that others might consider such an opinion mere motherly vanity. She wrote:

> Jennychen has striking dark hair and complexion and looks really fine with her childlike round, rosy cheeks and her deep, sweet eyes; Laura, some degrees brighter, lighter and clearer, is really prettier than her older sister because she has more regular features and because her sparkling greenish eyes, with their dark brows and long eyelashes, radiate a constant fire of joy. Both girls have figures of more than medium size and a very delicate shape . . . The third, the little one, is a real paragon of charm, grace and childish folly. She is the light and life of our house.[1]

The girls had become, in the course of time, real English ladies, hardly ever spoke German and felt that 'there was nothing more horrible than the thought of having to exchange England for Germany'.[2] Jenny did not want to return to her fatherland either, for while in the metropolis of London nobody paid any attention to what you thought or did, in

Germany everybody already knew the next morning 'how much income the master of the house has',[3] and Jenny would never have been able to answer that question.

When Karl returned at the end of Februrary 1869 with part of his paternal inheritance, Jenny's first thought was to leave their little terrace house in Grafton Terrace, where she and the children had experienced so much sadness. Some time ago she had discovered a large, elegant house not far from their own that was for rent. It had an imposing entrance, decorated with pillars in a pseudo-classic style, and the well-proportioned front hall led into a large parlour with a view of the park. On the first floor was a large room with a fireplace and likewise a pretty view of the park – an ideal study for Karl. Besides, there was a charming conservatory where, under Jennychen's special care, climbing plants were soon to bloom.

The move into 1 Modena Villas – also called 'Medina' – at the end of March 1864 meant the rise of the uncrowned leader of the communist movement from a bohemian existence to the lifestyle of a higher civil servant, doctor or lawyer. Engels called it 'the Medina [city of the apostle of God] of the emigration.' There the Marx family lived for eleven years; there the first book of the bible of communism, *Das Kapital*, saw the light of day; there the most important decisions of the International Workers' Association were taken; there Jennychen and Laura made the acquaintance of the young French revolutionaries whom they would later marry, much to their mother's sorrow. What worried Jenny was that her daughters would be exposed, as she herself was, 'to the anxieties and vexations that are the lot of all political women'.[4] For as she often said with a sigh: 'One would often like to turn away with disgust from all politics, and I wish we could look upon the whole field as pure "amateurs", but it is unfortunately for us always a matter of life and death.'[5]

For most of their friends politics was not a matter of life and death. They had either given it up and devoted themselves entirely to their professional duties, or they talked politics after the day's work, over a glass of beer. When Jenny thought about all the anxieties of her life, she felt that it was easy enough for Engels, a well-to-do textile manufacturer, to wait for revolutions and the dictatorship of the proletariat. It was depressing and unfair that Karl, who was working on the basic concepts of the new world order, was dependent on Engels for financial support. As the leader of the movement Karl deserved to get the necessary means for his livelihood and that of his family.

The long hoped-for paternal inheritance that Karl brought with him was not as high as he had hoped – since he had received several advances – but it amounted to about £700. In addition, he quite unexpectedly received another inheritance of almost the same amount. Their old, faithful party friend Wilhelm Wolff, 'Lupus', died in Manchester shortly after they had moved into Modena Villas. By giving private lessons and leading a very modest bachelor life he had saved a fortune of almost £1,000, the largest part of which he bequeathed to the Marx family.

As the owner of capital of almost £1,500, Marx, still working on a scientific refutation of the capitalist system, found himself suddenly in the company of small capitalists and did what would have greatly surprised his capitalist uncle Lion Philips, he 'speculated partly in American funds, but mainly in English shares that are appearing this year like mushrooms from the soil. I have made more than £400 this way and I am going to start once more. This kind of operation does not take much time and is worth the risk to confiscate the money of your enemies.'[6]

However, there is no mention later on of his making money by stock-exchange speculations. On the contrary, barely two years after his sudden acquisition of wealth he again had to ask Engels for money for rent and housekeeping. But during these two years there was a lot of fun in the Marx house.

In the autumn of 1864 Jenny could go on shopping sprees instead of queuing up at the pawnshop to pawn her dresses. In the large London stores she bought things for the house, herself and her daughters. At an auction she bought a carving knife and fork for Engels because her husband had told her that they were missing in Engels' household. That it was Engels to whom Jenny gave a knife and fork is not without a certain irony, for it was Engels, after all, who kept the knives and forks of the Marx family going. For herself and her daughters Jenny bought evening dresses, for she had decided to give a great ball to prove to her English friends and acquaintances that now, Jenny von Westphalen, the '*Ballkönigin*' of Trier, the belle of the ball, would also rule in the house of Marx. The English biographer of Marx, Robert Payne, assumes that somewhere in an old London chest there must still be a copy of the official, gold-rimmed invitation to a ball that Jenny sent to fifty friends and acquaintances:

Dr. Karl Marx
and Frau Dr. Jenny Marx
née von Westphalen
invite the pleasure of your
company
at a ball given at their residence

1, Modena Villas, Maitland Park, Haverstock Hill
London N.W.3
on October 12, 1864[7]

A dance band was hired and liveried servants offered choice food and wine. Jenny in her new ball dress and Karl in frock coat with his monocle on a ribbon, showed their daughters how one behaves in distinguished society.

It was a marvellous evening and Jenny reports that 'a few smaller parties followed after this small ball'.[8] She was now 50 years old. Her years of struggle for daily bread had made her weary and ill, but in her beautiful new house she now lived by the motto: Let the world perish nobly! Subconsciously she must have known that given their present lifestyle, their inherited money would soon be used up and there was no relying on royalty income, for even if Karl should finish his long-planned work, there was no certainty it would be a financial success. Hence she enjoyed her life to the full, went to the seaside for her health, attended concerts and the theatre and gave parties for her girls. For Tussy, who loved animals, a total of seven pets were acquired: two dogs, three cats and two birds.

One day, when Karl excitedly showed her a letter from Freiligrath with the news that Lassalle had lost his life in a duel, she at first shook her head incredulously. But in the end she thought it was better for the cause of the German worker that the poseur Lassalle was no longer the president of the General German Workers' Union, for she was convinced that only her husband had a right to that position. Marx, too, toyed with the idea of getting himself elected president of the GGWU at their next congress. When Liebknecht, who had returned to Germany with his family and held a leading position in the GGWU, asked him whether he would accept the presidency, Marx answered that this was impossible 'because I am still not permitted to reside in Prussia'.[9] On the other hand, he thought 'it would be a good demonstration by the party against the Prussian government as well as against the bourgeoisie, if the Workers' Congress elected me. I would then explain publicly why I could *not* accept the position'.[10] But nothing came of it. At the Congress of the GGWU Bernhard Becker, whom Lassalle had nominated, was elected President. Marx called him condescendingly 'an unfortunate fellow'.[11]

He himself assumed the leadership of the International Workers' Association (IWA) that had been founded by English and French workers and in October 1864 composed his *Inaugural Address*, which ends with the same famous appeal as *The Communist Manifesto*: 'Workers of the world unite!'

For years Marx did not shrink from time or effort to conduct the affairs of the First International. As a result of this activity his study in Maitland Park became the meeting place of many revolutionary socialists, young and old, and he was admired not only for being the prophet of scientific socialism, but for his active work towards its realization.

The workload he took upon himself with this double role of

thinker and doer was so great that his body rebelled again. 'My poor husband could hardly move for three weeks and was firmly attached to the sofa'.[12] Painful ulcers, carbuncles and furuncles, appeared everywhere on his body, even on his anus and penis, making it impossible for him to work. This meant that everybody in the family had to help the Moor as much as possible. His wife and his daughters, who worshipped their father, were more than willing to do that. The two oldest – Jennychen, now 20, and Laura, 19 – went to the British Museum for him and took notes from government reports on the economic conditions of the working classes, or wrote letters for him, while Jenny tried to ease the pain with soothing compresses.

Marx had hoped that his great work on political economy would be finished by the end of 1884, but as so often, he deceived himself. It took another three years before *Das Kapital* was published. For Jenny, who had great hopes for the appearance of the book, they were years of many surprises.

First there was a telegram from Engels in Manchester announcing the arrival of her brother Edgar from Texas. 'I have not seen him for sixteen long years', she wrote:

> Then came the sudden news. I thought my heart would burst with joy and happiness . . . Edgar was the ideal of my childhood and youth, my dear, my only companion. I clung to him with all my soul. My little Edgar was named after him . . . Then he arrives and is, alas, so changed, so sick, so miserable that I hardly recognize him. Only now, little by little, can I slowly recognize the old features in his face and see again the playmate of my childhood. He has taken part in the war in Texas for three years and has suffered beyond description; he lost everything, everything, including his health. He is now here to recover a bit; he will then go to Berlin to my brother and his other relatives and try his luck there! The poor boy! It is well known how rich, distinguished relatives are, especially if they are godfearing. One feels at such moments only what it means to be poor.[13]

Thus Jenny describes the appearance of her brother in a letter to Ernestine Liebknecht, who lived in Berlin with her husband William and their children. She added that she hoped the Liebknechts 'would receive Edgar kindly',[14] but she did not want him to get involved in any kind of politics, 'because it could spoil his relations with his relatives, upon whom he is dependent'.[15] She ends the letter with the English sentence 'that's a hint to you'.[16]

Marx looked upon the sudden appearance of his brother-in-law and former party comrade with mixed feelings. He called Edgar, who stayed six months with them, 'an expensive guest',[17] and wrote to Engels that it was 'a curious irony of fate that this Edgar, who never exploited anyone except himself, and who was always a workman in the strictest sense of the word, endured a war of, and with starvation for the slave-holders. Ditto that we two brothers-in-law are being ruined momentarily by the American War.'[18]

What annoyed Marx was that Edgar 'vegetated. He has even given up women and his sex drive has gone into his belly'.[19] But his daughters thought that their mother's brother was a good-natured, funny fellow and they listened attentively when he talked about Texas. They were not surprised that he wanted to go back and open a cigar and wine store 'with the obvious, cunning idea that he would thus be able to get hold of cigars and wine more easily.'[20]

Jenny's joy in her brother's presence was dampened by their rapidly eroding funds. Barely two years after their grand entrance into 'Medina', the housekeeping money was again so short that she was back at the pawnshop raising funds to feed her family and Edgar. She was relieved, therefore, when her brother went to Berlin in November and glad to hear that her rich relations had received the wrecked Texan in a friendly manner. They suggested that there might be a minor position for him in the civil service and gave him, as Jenny notes ironically, 'a hymn book as a Christmas present',[21] in order to reintroduce the heathen into the circle of his pious relatives.

Shortly after Edgar's departure, Marx too left London to discuss some basic questions of the International Workers'

Association with Engels. While they hatched plots and carried on highly political conversations in Manchester – 'in the next revolution, which is perhaps closer than it looks now, *we* (i.e. you and I) will have this powerful instrument (the International) in our hands'[22] – the landlord appeared and threatened Jenny with the bailiff, if he did not get his rent soon. 'I found my wife in such a desolate state of mind that I did not have the courage to explain to her the true state of things.'[23] The true state of things was that there was no housekeeping money, 'and yet we simply must get coal'.[24]

Once again Engels came to the rescue. He sent £15 and as a tonic for Jennychen, who was sick again, a case of port, sherry and claret. Keeping up the façade became particularly difficult in the ensuing years because many of the young men in the International became fond of the pretty daughters of the leader of the movement: Laura especially was surrounded by suitors. On 1 May 1865, the twenty-first birthday of her sister Jenny, she received a marriage proposal from a wealthy young South American, whose sisters were friends of hers. But she rejected it firmly, because she did not love the young man. The disappointed lover thereupon put Laura's picture into a jewelled locket. Her mother thought the gesture was touching and could not understand why it annoyed Laura. It was but a small sign that Jenny's relationship to her politically engaged daughters was becoming more distant.

Laura wrote to her sister that she was horrified when her mother suddenly appeared one day, while she was having a long earnest conversation with a young man: 'Mama came in without her boots on and wearing just enough that one did not have to rely on the naked effect of nature and yet dressed in such a way that she showed more than she veiled. You know how sensitive our friend is and how easily he blushes. He was fully justified. For my part, I simply closed my eyes and did not look where I could not look without blushing or blanching.'[25]

On the other hand, the relationship of the daughters to their father, dear 'Challey', 'Master', 'Moor', or 'Old Nick', which had been close to begin with, became even closer as time went by. They admired his astuteness, his humour and his sarcastic wit. They watched with interest the slow development of *Das Kapital* and rejoiced when it was finally finished, that 'this nightmare, your book, is no longer resting on your shoulders'.[26]

Laura wrote to her father in April 1867, when he had gone to his publisher Meissner in Hamburg with the manuscript of the first volume of *Das Kapital* and was spending a few weeks in Germany: 'It must be a great feeling to get rid of all this petty family business for a while, to say nothing of the company you keep. I have noticed that a certain lady is often mentioned in your letters. Is she young? Is she clever? Is she pretty? Are you flirting with her or do you allow her to flirt with you? You seem to admire her greatly and it would be *trop bête* to assume that all the admiration is only on your side. I would be jealous, if I were Mama.'[27]

Jenny was not jealous, for she accepted the fact that the moral code of men differed from that of women. She writes that when the copied manuscript of *Das Kapital* was lying in front of her 'a giant load was taken off my mind; yet there still remain enough worries and burdens, especially with the girls falling in love, getting engaged to Frenchmen, even medical students.'[28]

At first Marx was not very happy either with Laura's engagement to the medical student Paul Lafargue, who had a Creole grandmother. Before giving his consent to the engagement that both young people wanted, he demanded from his future son-in-law in a long letter written in French – Lafargue spoke neither English nor German – a precise report on the financial conditions of the Lafargue family. He also warned the young man, who was passionately in love with Laura, that he would have to give up his manner of courting, since true love is shown by the restraint and modesty of the lover toward his idol. Jenny must have smiled inwardly when she heard this, for she remembered very well the passionate embraces of her little black boar. Marx probably did not show her a passage in his letter to Lafargue which expresses a tragic truth: 'You know that I have devoted my entire fortune to the revolutionary struggle. I do not regret it. On the contrary, I would do the same if I had to start my life again. But I would not marry. As far as it lies in my power, I shall protect my daughter from the cliffs upon which her mother's life was wrecked.'[29]

In reply to Marx's long letter, Lafargue's father wrote from Bordeaux that he would always support his son financially and that Paul would first have to pass his medical school examinations in London and in Paris before he could think of marrying. Jenny breathed a sigh of relief. Writing to her friend Ernestine Liebknecht, she said: 'Fortunately, he does not depend on his practice, which is always difficult at the beginning. His parents are well-to-do; they own plantations and property in Santiago and Bordeaux, and since Paul is their only child he will inherit everything. They have behaved very generously toward Laura, have received her like a daughter with open arms and have promised to give the young couple 1,000 francs on their wedding day.'[30] Jenny also emphasized that Paul had the same ideals as Laura, which she considered important for her daughter's happiness, 'particularly concerning religion. Thus Laura will avoid the inevitable conflicts and sorrows that a girl with her convictions experiences in bourgeois society'.[31] She meant that Laura had learned from her father to consider religion as 'the opium of the people' and that Lafargue was an atheist, too. Although Jenny had become an atheist like her husband, the questions of religion occupied her all her life. What annoyed her was the sanctimoniousness of the English bourgeoisie, the hypocritical routine of going to church every Sunday, 'but the dear Lord God continued to appear in her mouth and pen, whether she liked it or not, although he had long since lost his place of honour in her heart'.[32] She was proud when the Cunninghams, 'a well-known aristocratic family',[33] asked Laura and Jenny to be the bridesmaids at the wedding of their daughter, and did not worry that this meant that the girls had to go into a church – on the contrary, for she remembered her own church wedding with nostalgia. However, there was no question of a church wedding for Laura, and her civil marriage had to be repeatedly postponed because her parents had no money for it. Karl tried in vain to get a loan from his rich Dutch relatives, but the inevitable solution was yet another £5 note from Engels. Jenny breathed a sigh of relief, for the marriage meant two less mouths to feed.

Jenny's hopes for the commercial success of *Das Kapital* and the revolutionary transformation of society kept her buoyant, as did Engels' optimism: Engels encouraged her in this hope. 'In a fortnight the fun begins in Prussia',[34] he wrote in June 1866. 'If this chance is lost without being used, and if the people put up with it, we might just as well pack up our revolutionary bags and concentrate on higher theory'.[35] And in September 1867, when the higher theory finally appeared in the form of the first volume of *Das Kapital*, it met with a complete lack of comprehension. There were only a few notices in the German press, even counting the extensive reviews Marx and Engels wrote themselves and submitted anonymously. And Marx's request for numerous review copies of his book was rejected by his publisher. Jenny, too, tried to promote her husband's book. In a long letter, published by Johann Philip Becker, a friend and the Swiss editor of the newspaper *Der Vorbote*, she writes:

> Let me advise you, if you already have a copy of the book by Karl Marx, if you have not worked your way through the dialectic subtleties of the first parts, as I have, read those that deal with the original accumulation of capital and the modern theory of colonization. I am convinced that you will be in complete agreement with them, as I am. Of course, Marx does not have a specific remedy on hand – for which the bourgeois world, which also now calls itself socialistic, clamours – no pills, no ointment, no lint to cure the gaping, bleeding wounds of our society; but it seems to me that, from the historic process of development of modern society, he has brought the practical results and applications to their boldest conclusions and that it was no mean feat to lift up the

astonished philistine, by means of statistical facts and dialectic manoeuvres, to the dizzying height of these sentences: 'Violence is the midwife of any old society that is pregnant with a new one. It is itself an economic force . . . much of the capital that appears today in the United States without any birth certificate was capital accumulated from the blood of English children . . . If money comes into the world with blood on its cheeks, then capital is oozing blood and grime from head to foot from all pores'. Or the whole passage: 'The sands of capitalistic private property are running out', etc. to the end.

I must honestly confess that the simple pathos of this passage has moved me and that the whole matter is now as clear as sunlight.[36]

This review, written by Jenny with verve and conviction, would have been more effective if it had appeared in a larger paper. *Der Vorbote*, a Geneva monthly, was well known as the organ of the International, but it had few readers in Germany. Marx knew that one 'must make a noise' to sell books and he tried it often enough, but unsuccessfully. It is said that only two hundred copies of *Das Kapital* were sold during the first year of its publication. Hence there was no royalty income and the bailiff was soon back banging on the door. Jenny was once again left hopeless and without resources. 'My wife has pawned everything and can hardly go out now',[37] wrote Marx to Engels.

At the end of 1868 Engels enquired how great Marx's debts were and if he could live on £350 a year. Engels himself was about to sell his share of the firm Ermen & Engels to his partner and retire from the textile business, but because he knew that the head of the International could not exist without his financial support, he demanded an annual pension for Marx, in addition to his own compensation agreement.

Marx was overwhelmed by Engels' generous offer, which would relieve him of his eternal money worries. In his reply he describes

how unpleasant matters have become here in the past few months, as can be seen from the fact that Jennychen has accepted a position

– behind my back – as a tutor in an English family. Although I found the whole matter very unfortunate (the child has to teach little children almost all day long) – I don't have to tell you about that – I agreed to it only on the stipulation that the engagement was only binding for a month, because I thought it was good for Jennychen to be distracted by any kind of occupation and to get out of these four walls. My wife has been in a hysterical state for years – understandable from the circumstances but for that reason not more pleasant – and is torturing the children to death with her lamentations, crankiness and ill humour, although no children could bear it in a more jolly way.[38]

The assertion that Jenny had been 'torturing her children to death for years' is certainly exaggerated; it is true that she had been physically and mentally destroyed by the daily worries that she had to endure for years and that she was often very brusque with her girls, because she had to hide the family's true financial condition from them. Engels' offer of a regular pension rescued her from the depressing uncertainty of her present life.

II

Jenny witnessed the endless contentious discussions, often lasting into the early morning hours, that her husband carried on with various representatives of workers' associations in order to give the International clear guidelines. They were not always precisely followed. Even such an old friend of Marx's as Wilhelm Liebknecht, a member of the General German Workers' Union, had to put up with a lot of criticism; he was, as Jenny called it, too 'wishy-washy'. She was annoyed that 'Wilhelmchen' did not have the courage to divert the General German Workers' Union from Lassalle's heresy of an evolutionary socialism to her husband's brand of revolutionary communism; after all, the entire concept of workers' unions owed its existence to Karl. She wished that Karl would emphasize his position more strongly as chief ideologue of the

International and regretted that he had appointed that German tailor Eccarius to the secretaryship of the General Council of the International.

When Karl was too ill to attend to all his political correspondence personally, Jenny would answer for him. In February 1866, for example, there appeared in *Der Verbote* an excerpt from 'A London Letter', in which Jenny reports on a 'significant movement'[39] taking place 'in stagnant England concerning religion'.[40] It involves

> extremely enlightened, indeed truly bold lectures given to the people by the top men of science, with Huxley at the head, on Sunday evenings, precisely at the hour when the flock normally makes its pilgrimage to the meadow of the Lord; the hall was filled to the rafters and the rejoicing of the people so loud that 2,000 people could not get into the overcrowded hall on the first Sunday evening, when I was there with my family. The priests permitted the terrible thing to happen three times. Last night the assembly was told that no lectures could be given anymore, until the suit of the ministers against the 'Sunday Evenings for the People' had been settled. There was a spontaneous outcry of indignation by the assembly and more than £100 were collected to carry on the suit. How stupid of the priesthood to start it.[41]

In this published letter Jenny mentions that it was a sign of the times that 'the English working class has great sympathy for the cause of the Fenians'.[42] She might have added that in the Marx family, too, the cause of the Fenians – a secret society founded in America by Irish emigrants to free Ireland from the British yoke – met with deep sympathy.

Marx considered the Irish freedom fighters allies in the coming revolution against their capitalistic oppressors and for Engels, whose new mistress was Lizzy Burns, the sister of the deceased Mary Burns, the cause of Ireland was a matter dear to his heart. He started writing a book on the history of Ireland. When the attempt of some Fenians living in Manchester to free one of their arrested comrades from a paddy wagon cost an English policeman his life, five of the Fenians involved were arrested and condemned to death. The sentence caused a wave of protests in Ireland and America and was also condemned by the General Council of the International. Marx declared: 'The political executions in Manchester bring to mind the fate of John Brown in Harper's Ferry. They are the start of a new phase in the struggle between England and Ireland'.[43]

To educate the people on the Continent as to the fate of the Fenians imprisoned by the British government, Marx and Jennychen wrote accusatory articles in French for *La Marseillaise*, a paper associated with the International. Jennychen published a long letter by O'Donovan Rossa, the co-founder of the society of Fenians in Ireland and editor of the *Irish People*, who was sentenced to life imprisonment in England. She describes how he was thrown into a dark cell, his hands tied behind his back. 'They did not take his hand-fetters off either by day or night so that he had to eat his food, a liquid porridge, by lying on the floor.'[44] After mentioning a number of other Irish martyrs, she ends with the sentence: 'I could add many names to this list. Suffice it to say that since 1866, when the office of the *Irish People* was raided, twenty Fenians have died or gone crazy in the dungeons of philanthropic England'.[45] When the news came that the peasants of Tipperary had elected the imprisoned O'Donovan to the House of Commons, they danced for joy in the Marx house. 'Tussy was exuberant'[46] and Jenny was delighted by the concern the election caused in the English press: 'A convicted criminal has been elected – oh horror of horrors'.[47]

Among Marx's German admirers was a respected gynaecologist, Dr Ludwig Kugelmann, who kept an elegant house in Hanover and frequented the best circles but had been an enthusiast of communism since his student days. He was one of the few readers of *Das Kapital* who really studied it and maintained close personal ties with Marx and his family. In April 1867, when Marx had gone to his Hamburg publisher Meissner with the first volume of *Das Kapital*, Kugelmann had asked him to come to Hanover for a visit. To his surprise Marx noted that Kugelmann had in his library 'a more complete collection of our writings than we have ourselves'.[48] He wrote to Engels that Kugelmann was 'a fanatic . . . supporter of our doctrine and of ourselves. He annoyed me occasionally with his enthusiasm, which contrasts with his professional coldness.'[49]

In the Kugelmann's family living room were several busts of the classical gods, among them one of Jupiter which, Kugelmann thought, looked like Marx. He sent it to London in 1867 as a Christmas present and a token of his admiration for Marx. A surprised Jenny wrote him: 'You cannot imagine what joy and surprise you gave us yesterday. I really do not know how to thank you for your friendship and sympathy and now especially for the latest sign of your concern, the godly Father Zeus, who will now take the place of Father Christmas with us'.[50] She told him how she had been down in the kitchen with Lenchen and her girls making thorough preparation for the Christmas pudding, when the bell rang:

> A cab stops in front of the house, mysterious steps are going back and forth, there is a whispering and murmuring in the house, and suddenly a voice comes from upstairs: 'A big statue has arrived'. If they had shouted: fire, fire the house is on fire, the Fenians have come, we could not have rushed up more confused, more stunned, and there it stood in front of our eyes in all its colossal magnificence, its ideal purity the old Jupiter tonans, undamaged, intact!! . . . Then the debates began at once where the most dignified niche was for the new 'dear God who art in heaven and on earth'.[51]

Marx himself was much more grateful to Kugelmann for getting some of Engels' reviews of *Das Kapital*, written under various pseudonyms, placed in German newspapers. While Jenny openly expressed her joy at the present, Marx wrote only: 'My best thanks for the Jupiter and for your activity and interest in making propaganda and a fool of the German press'.[52]

When Kugelmann urged him to finish the second volume of *Das Kapital*, Marx told him that he had been ill almost all winter and unable to work and that he considered it necessary 'quickly to learn some Russian, because it has become un-avoidable to study Russian landed property rights in their original sources, when I treat the land question'.[53] Jenny worried that her sick husband 'instead of taking care of himself was studying Russian come hell or high water',[54] and when he showed her a carbuncle under his arm only after it was very swollen and hardened, she wrote to Engels: 'I have secretly wished for years that you were here, dear Mr Engels. Many things would be different.'[55] But then she got alarmed and asked Engels not to mention this in his letters to Marx. 'He is so easily irritated now and would feel annoyed. But it was such a relief for me to pour out my heart to you, because I am quite powerless to change anything in his way of life'.[56]

Engels had often asked himself, after finishing his years as a textile manufacturer, whether he should not move closer to his friend. In response to Jenny's letter he asked her to help him find a house in their neighbourhood. So, jointly with her two daughters, Jenny and Tussy, she set out on a 'journey of discovery' and hastened to 'give a report'[57] to Engels. 'I have now found a house that pleases us very much because of its wonderful, open situation . . . It lies close to Primrose Hill so that all the front rooms have a magnificent, unhampered view and fresh air'.[58] She then describes it in detail. It has a very spacious bathroom with a large bathtub, a deep basement that 'could become a very useful cool wine cellar. There are two very pleasant rooms on the ground floor, separated by double doors, the back one having a particularly attractive green-house. On the first floor in front, a very beautiful, large room and next to it a smaller one. On the second floor 3 bedrooms. I doubt whether you could find a better house and feel sure that your wife will like it.'[59] Engels' 'wife' was, of course, his mistress Lizzie: Jenny had ambivalent feelings about her pre-decessor and sister Mary, but she liked Lizzie and was happy, therefore, that her efforts to find a house for them in their neighbourhood proved successful. The last and closest phase of co-operation between Marx and Engels dates from 1870, when Engels moved to the house Jenny had found them in Regent's Park Road.

Unanticipated political and military events on the Continent, the Franco–Prussian war and the bloody suppression of the Paris Commune, were the heralds of this phase. The head of the International was very disappointed that 'the rustic squire Bismarck' had succeeded in bringing about what people had been on the barricades for in 1848 – the unification of Germany. It was an even greater disappointment that the German workers welcomed the monarchy enthusiastically, instead of fighting for the republic. Marx reflected secretly whether he would have been able to influence these developments by accepting Bismarck's offer: 'Marx should make use of his considerable talents in the interest of the German people.'[60] But it was much too late for that now.

Jenny, who followed the Franco–Prussian war with mixed feelings, was not keen on returning to her fatherland. She read with great interest Engels' series of articles 'On the War' that appeared in the *Pall Mall Gazette*. 'I cannot help it, I must call you the young Moltke',[61] she told him. But while her daughters sympathized with the French, she was of the opinion that the French 'deserve the Prussian thrashing, for all Frenchmen, even the few better ones, are chauvinists in the deepest recesses of their hearts. Their chauvinism is being knocked out of them.'[62]

It soon became apparent, however, that the French were not the only ones who had chauvinistic feelings. Patriotic pride filled German hearts as a result of the quick defeat of the French armies. When it became known that Napoleon III was taken prisoner in the battle of Sedan on 2 September 1870, a wave of patriotic enthusiasm swept through all classes of the German people.

Appeals by the International, which Marx prepared in all-night meetings, tried to persuade the workers of both peoples not to use their arms against each other, but against their exploiters. In the first address of the General Council of the International concerning the Franco–Prussian war, written by

Marx in July 1870 and sent to all members of the International, he said: 'In a meeting of shop stewards in Chemnitz, representing 50,000 Saxon workers, the following resolution was passed unanimously: We declare in the name of German Democracy and in particular of the workers of the Social Democratic Party, that the present war is exclusively a dynastic war . . . Mindful of the motto of the International, "Workers of the World Unite", we shall never forget that the workers of all countries are our friends and the despots of all countries our enemies.'[63]

When in March 1871, at the end of the war they had lost, the workers of Paris went onto the barricades and proclaimed the Commune, which was soon brutally suppressed, Marx lost no time in informing the members of the International in a further address 'Concerning the General Tendency of the Struggle'. In this brilliantly written piece that concludes with the words: 'The Paris of the workers and its Commune will be honoured forever as the glorious herald of a new social order',[64] he protested emphatically against the 'police-coloured bourgeois mind'[65] that considers the International a secret society, whose 'General Council orders uprisings in various countries from time to time'.[66]

To his surprise this address caused a much greater sensation than all his previous books or articles. He was denounced by French papers as '*le grand Chef de l'Internationale*' and English papers too warned against him. He informed his friend Kugelmann: 'I have the honour of being at this time the most slandered and most threatened man in London . . . This is something to be grateful for after twenty years of a rustic idyll'.[67]

His family, however, was not at all happy about his sudden fame, for they feared that the English government would expel the defender of the 'Parisian Perpetrators of Murder and Arson' – as the Communards were called. According to the pro-government paper *The Observer*, legal steps against Marx were being considered. Nothing came of that, but when the Monroes, an English family, whose children Jennychen Marx tutored, heard, 'that I am the daughter of the Chief-Arsonist, who defends the cursed commune movement, they severed all relations with me'.[68] A massive hate campaign organized by the French government and finding expression in leading articles in all the major British newspapers, was responsible for a sharp condemnation of the International. One example: 'The Internationalists in London are no less serious than their brethren in Paris in their insistence that the old society has to perish and should perish. They proclaim the burning of public buildings and the shooting of hostages as "a gigantic effort to overthrow society which, even though it is not always successful, will be continued, until the aim has been achieved".'[69] Marx and Engels tried to refute these and other accusations by writing letters to the editors of many papers, but without success.

The English public considered the International a dangerous organization, whose leader belonged in jail. In June 1871, the *Pall Mall Gazette* published the rumour that Marx had been arrested in Holland. The following day Marx replied: 'While I imagine I am living in London, I note from your Parisian correspondence in yesterday's edition, that I have been arrested in Holland at the request of Bismarck-Favre.'[70] Jenny, however, was worried and wrote: 'The Moor is all right. These are all police lies. You have no idea how much misery and anger we have experienced in these weeks. It took more than twenty years to train these brave, capable and heroic men and now they are all dead.'[71] The death of Gustave Florens, a young Frenchmen close to her, touched Jenny deeply. In an obituary, published in the *Volksstaat*, she wrote:

We have all been affected most deeply by the death of Gustave Florens. He was our friend and a very noble soul. Bold to audacity, chivalrous, humane, compassionate, soft to weakness (nothing human was alien to him), with a richly endowed mind, a scholar and a representative of modern science; young, rich, and with pleasant, agreeable manners he devoted his warm, impulsive nature to the poor, the oppressed, the disinherited, not only to those fighting and struggling in his own country, no, his great heart beat for every nation, every race, every tribe . . . He was the red spectre that the bourgeoisie saw incorporated in him and persecuted with raging fury . . . I fear, I fear, the communist movement, the first ray of dawn in the darkness, is lost.[72]

In addition to the worry that the communist movement was lost as a result of the bloody events in Paris, came the worry about the future of the International. Marx had to struggle from the beginning against the opinions of some groups in the International about the road towards communism. His fiercest opponent was the anarchist Mikhail Bakunin, who considered the proclamation of the dictatorship of the proletariat dangerous because it violated, like any dictatorship, the human right of freedom. He wrote: 'I regret the blindness of those who believe that they can achieve economic equality and justice in any other way except by freedom. Equality without freedom is a terrible fiction, created by swindlers to mislead fools. Equality without freedom means state despotism.'[73]

Marx, who considered the dictatorship of the proletariat the necessary first phase towards the establishment of a communist society, condemned such ideas as a betrayal of the International. He tried to convince like-minded comrades by using all the tricks of insinuation and character-assassination, that it was necessary to expel Bakunin and his followers from the International. In the name of the General Council of the International, he drew up, together with Engels, detailed denunciations of the lie that had been published in newspapers favourable to Bakunin, that 'the General Council was a committee of Germans headed by a Bismarckian brain.'[74] In long letters to friends and sympathizers Jenny never tired of declaring that the Moor had carried on the almost unbearable workload of the International for years and nobody had taken any notice of it and now, 'when his enemies have put his name in the limelight, the whole mob gets together and policemen and democrats howl the same refrain of "despotism, authoritarianism, ambition"'! He would feel so much better if he had been able to continue working quietly preparing the theory of their struggle for the fighters. But no peace, day or night! And how ruinous for our private lives, what a gêne [torture]! Just at a time when our girls needed help.'[75]

That they needed their parents' help would hardly have occurred to the Marx daughters. Laura was in France with her husband, who had given up the medical profession and was now the emissary of the International. Her two sisters visited her shortly after the collapse of the Paris Commune, much to their mother's justified concern, for it became apparent very soon, that the daughters of the leader of the International were under close surveillance by the French police and were even arrested in the end.

While her daughters were caught up in their father's battles, Jenny wrote:

> In all these battles we women have to bear the hardest, i.e. pettiest, part. In the battle with the world the man gets stronger, stronger too in the face of his enemies, even if their number is legion; we sit at home and darn socks. That does not banish the worries, and little daily cares slowly but surely gnaw away the courage to face life. I am talking from more than thirty years' experience and I can say that I did not give up courage easily. But I have grown too old to have much hope, and the last unfortunate events have shocked me greatly. I am afraid that we, we older ones, won't live to see many good things'.[76]

12

Retired Revolutionaries

The failure of the Paris Commune led to one of the great turning-points in the life of Marx and his family. The time was obviously not yet ripe for the establishment of a communist order of society. For Marx this meant that the theoretical reasons for its inevitability simply had to be more convincingly stated. He planned to do this in a second, revised edition of the first volume of *Das Kapital* and continue it in a second volume. But because of the constant quarrels within the International, in which he was perforce involved, he did not have time for serious work.

After long discussions with Engels he decided to resign his position as Head of the International at the convention planned for The Hague in September 1872 – but only if the followers of Bakunin were prevented from taking over the control of the General Council. 'The life and death of the International are at stake at the International Congress (The Hague opens September 2) and before I resign I shall try to protect it from disruptive elements',[1] Marx wrote to Kugelmann, whom he offered a mandate as a delegate in the hope that he would attend the Congress and vote for him. Kugelmann came and did as he was told, although he disliked international political meetings.

His daughter reported that her father met Mrs Marx for the first time in The Hague: 'a slender, almost youthful-looking woman, who was passionately interested in all party affairs, indeed totally engrossed in them',[2] and went on to hint darkly that Jenny's influence was baleful – 'Some time ago Jennychen said, without mentioning any names: "Unfortunately, somebody is driving the Moor to this agitation; one could hate her for that".'[3] But it would be ridiculous to hold Jenny responsible for Karl's political activities. He was his own master and nobody, not even his wife, could divert him from his chosen path. How strong his will was became apparent at The Hague congress, where he succeeded in expelling the very popular Bakunin from the International.

In his personal life, Marx was no less determined, as the next incident reveals. Among the French communards who had fled to London there were two who visited the Head of the International, not only because they sought his advice but because they were attracted to his two daughters, Jennychen and Tussy. The younger of the two, Charles Longuet, the former editor of the socialist paper *La Rive Gauche*, was no stranger. He had been associated with the Marx family in 1866, when his friend Paul Lafargue married Laura Marx. He now fell in love with Jennychen (who reciprocated) and duly received permission from her parents to marry him in 1872. But the other communard, likewise a French journalist, was Prosper Olivier Lissagaray, a Count by birth who had given up his title because of his revolutionary convictions. He was 34 years old, highly intelligent and actively engaged in editing the magazine *Rouge et Noir*. He had come to Marx to get advice concerning the translation of his book *Histoire de la Commune de 1871* into English and German. Marx was greatly interested in this project and personally supervised the translation into German.

The English translation was done by his 17-year-old daughter Tussy, who fell passionately in love with the author of the book in the course of her work. Lissagaray, over-whelmed by the spontaneity of Tussy's love, embraced her as *'ma petite femme'*.[4] But when it became known in the Marx family that Tussy and Lissa (as she called him) were engaged, Marx declared categorically that an engagement was out of the question: Lissagaray should first show what he could achieve in life, before thinking about marrying his daughter. Tussy suffered so much from her father's objection that she became ill – or rather, like her mother, fled into illness. To help her get over it, Marx took her on a visit to Brighton. When he left a few days later to go to Manchester, Tussy stayed on in Brighton and tried to support herself by giving private lessons. The sudden departure of her youngest daughter was so painful to Jenny that she went to visit her in Brighton, where she discovered to her surprise that Lissagaray, who was supposed to be in London, was in fact in Brighton too, and often in Tussy's company. She knew how angry Karl would be if he knew this and advised Tussy to come back home and wait for her father to agree to her engagement. She herself was willing to declare publicly that Tussy and Lissagaray were engaged. Tussy returned to London and waited. On 23 March 1874, she wrote her beloved father a letter of moving and revealing simplicity:

My dearest Moor,
I would like to ask you for something now, but you must first promise not to get angry. I would like to know, dear Moor, when I may see L. again. It is *very* hard *never* to see him. I have really tried to be patient, but it is so very hard and I feel I cannot stand it any longer. I do not expect you to say that he may come here. I do not wish that myself, but could I not go for a walk with him now and again? You have permitted me to go for walks with Outin and Frankel. Why not with him? Nobody will be surprised to see us together, because everybody knows that we are engaged . . .

When I was very sick in Brighton (during one week I fainted two or three times every day), L. came to visit me and every time I felt stronger and happier. I could then more easily bear the heavy workload lying on my shoulders. It has been so long since I have been together with him, and I am so miserable, although I am honestly trying to be cheerful and happy. But I cannot do it anymore. Please believe me, dear Moor, if I could see him now and again, it would do me more good than all Mrs. Anderson's medicine. I am sure of it.

In any case, dearest Moor, if I may not see him *now*, tell me please, *when* I may see him. It would be something to look forward to and it would be less difficult to wait, if it were not as indefinite as now. My dearest Moor, please do not be angry with me for having written this and forgive me, if I cause you concern.
Your Tussy[5]

Marx repressed the sentence 'nobody will be surprised to see us together because everybody knows that we are engaged', since the thought of an engagement between Tussy and Lissagaray was unbearable to him. Perhaps he wanted to protect his beloved seventeen-year-old daughter from a man twice her age; or perhaps he, like Jenny, did not wish a Frenchman as his third son-in-law. But, whatever his reasons for rejecting the man Tussy loved passionately and whose fiancée she remained for ten years, it was to have tragic consequences in Tussy's later life. The positive side of this was that his youngest daughter – Jenny called her 'a politician from head to toe'[6] – remained at home and helped her father, of whom she said 'nobody can know how much I love him'.[7]

In the following years Marx's main work, often interrupted by illnesses, was the second volume of *Das Kapital*. He never finished it. Accompanied by Tussy, he travelled several times to Karlsbad for the cure, where he moved in the best circles, observed but unmolested by the police. The ladies of Karlsbad society were surprised when they learned that the dignified elderly gentleman with a monocle and wearing a tailor-made English suit, was the patriarch of the workers. One of the ladies once remarked to him: 'I cannot imagine you living in a classless time because you have aristrocratic preferences and habits',[8] to which he is supposed to have answered, 'I cannot either. Those times will come, but we must be gone by then.'[9]

In the last years of her life Jenny was afflicted by both

physical and mental pain. It hurt her that her three daughters –
the two married ones, Laura and Jenny, but Tussy also – had a
much stronger bond with their father than with her. When
Marx went to Karlsbad for the cure with Tussy, she stayed
home or went alone or with Lizzy to Ramsgate or some other
English seaside resort. Only once, in 1877, when Karl was
about to go to Karlsbad again on the advice of his doctor, he
wrote to Engels: 'I intend to start for *Neuenahr* and not
Karlsbad, if possible on August 12th, for the following reasons:
first, because of the cost; you know that my wife is suffering
badly from impaired digestion, and since, in any case, I am
taking Tussy, who also had a painful attack again, my wife
would be greatly offended if she had to stay behind.'[10] Jenny
would probably not have been offended, for she had long
since accepted the fact that Karl did what he wanted to do.
Besides, she had established her own way of life. She took
care of her grandchildren, liked to go to the theatre and went
often, and gave Shakespeare recitations as she had done as a
girl.

Her father had introduced her to the world of Shakespeare
and now, as her life was approaching its end, it was to
Shakespeare she looked again. She was so much impressed by
the performance of a young English actor, Henry Irving, as
Hamlet that she wrote a critical review of it, which Tussy gave
to a correspondent of the *Frankfurter Zeitung*: 'It would be
wonderful if you could get Mama's review published in the
Frankfurter . . . Mama asks me to tell you she does not wish
her name to appear in the *Frankfurter*, but if you want to
indicate who has written the review, you may do so "among
friends".'[11] The review was published and several others
followed. One of the last she wrote, which was published in
the *Frankfurter Zeitung* in February 1877, begins with an
ironic introduction, in very much Marx's own style, about
the 'collapse' of the International Conference in Constanti-
nople because of Turkey's refusal to grant autonomy to
Hercegovina, Bulgaria, etc. 'The trumpet of war is silent and
the philistine blathering about politics, quietly puts his fearful

mind at rest, slumbers peacefully and lulls himself into golden dreams of peace and prosperity'.[12]

Then she describes the great event of the week, the performance of Shakespeare's *Richard III* given before an English public for the first time in the complete and original text. The play disappeared from the stage for half a century after Shakespeare's death; it was later performed in a mutilated version. But now Irving had the courage to perform the play 'as it was written': 'The great mass of people who besieged the doors of the Lyceum last Monday, proved how successful the experiment was. Immediately after the first monologue of Glou[ce]ster

> Now is the winter of our discontent
> Made glorious summer by this sun of York

the silence was breathless and even the gods of paradise listened in magic enchantment.'[13]

The cycle closed with Shakespeare. Jenny Marx spent most of the last years of her life in bed. Her illness was not dyspepsia, as the doctors diagnosed, but liver cancer and no medicines could help her, although she was given many. Like her, Karl was bound to his bed at the same time; he lay in the back room, she in the front. And then on 2 December 1881, 'when she felt that the moment of death had come, she called: "Karl, my strength is gone". These were her last lucid words. She was buried on 5 December at the cemetery of Highgate in the section of the damned'.[14] Her husband was too ill to pay his last respects, but Friedrich Engels delivered a short eulogy at her graveside.

Postscript

A few days before Jenny died, Marx received the December issue of the monthly review *Modern Thought* which had a long article about him and his work. 'The first English publication that shows real enthusiasm for new ideas and boldly confronts the British philistines. This is not to deny that most of the biographical data given about me by the authors is false.'[1] Marx also thought that the presentation of his basic economic thought and the quotations from *Kapital* were false or confused. However, in spite of these shortcomings 'the appearance of this article, which was announced by boldly lettered posters on the walls of the West-end of London, has caused a sensation. As far as I am concerned the best thing about all this was that I received the issue of *Modern Thought* on November 30th, so that my dear wife was cheered up in the last days of her life.'[2]

Since Marx himself praises this first attempt at presenting his ideas to a larger public, but at the same time criticizes the remarks made about him and his life, it is not surprising that many attempts made since then to show Karl Marx as he was have been condemned on party political grounds.

When Marx's son-in-law, Charles Longuet, published an obituary of Jenny in the Parisian paper *Justice*, in which he said that Jenny had to overcome many prejudices to marry the son of a Jewish lawyer and that racial prejudice was the strongest of all, Marx replied: 'This whole story is a *complete fabrication*, there were *no prejudices to overcome* . . . Longuet would do me a great favour if he were never again to mention my name in his writings.'[3] However, even if seriously meant, it was a wish that could not be fulfilled, for how can one write about the communist world movement without mentioning the name of Karl Marx? The pyramid of books about him has grown so large in the hundred-odd years since his death in 1883 that it is hard to estimate their number. The reader who approaches this pyramid without preconceptions gets the impression of a man like Schiller's Wallenstein:

> Distorted by the parties fear or favour
> What man he really was, we do not know

During the seven years of my efforts to understand the life of Jenny Marx there were times when I felt that it could not be done, because so many personal documents, letters and diaries, had been destroyed or were being withheld. Since I did not want to present an ideological thesis, I decided to lay out the facts about her life with her husband and her children, as she herself gave them. Even this was not easy, for Jenny often alludes to events without saying what happened. Still, I am convinced that the picture of Jenny Marx given here is basically correct. She lived in the shadow of a giant whose words and actions are still affecting us all for better or worse and only intimate party comrades knew what that meant in terms of Jenny's human happiness. Some referred to it poetically while applauding her husband's call to arms. The following lines about her were read in 1899 at the anniversary reunion of the Karl Marx classes of Boston, Massachusetts:

> Nor forget his companion, who, in tender affection,
> By the side of her dead whom love could not save,
> With no casket, no money in death's dark affliction
> To protect against want or the mould of the grave,
> Though thy name does not mingle with saints or with angels,
> The reign of thy virtue, sweet Jenny, we claim.
> And with tribute to Marx join the friendship of Engels,
> Though a tear dims the eye as we murmur thy name.

Acknowledgements

I would like to thank all those who have helped me with this work by answering the many questions I asked them. Here I am thinking above all of Jürgen Rojan, the Director of the Central European Department of the Internationaal Instituut voor Sociale Geschiedenis in Amsterdam, and of the librarian of the Karl-Marx-Museum in Trier, Dr Karl König. In England I owe thanks to Mrs Ivonne Kapp, author of the two-volume work on *Eleanor Marx*, my former student Denys Clark, to the Thames Water Authority for specific information concerning the sanitary conditions of the Marx homes in Dean Street and Grafton Terrace and also the librarian of the Royal Society of Health. I am indebted to my colleague Professor Charles White, for drawing my attention to the poem on Jenny Marx. In the library of my own university – Portland State University – two people have given me much help during my long efforts to understand Jenny Marx: Evelyn Crowell, responsible for inter-library loans and, last but not least, our librarian Elmer Magnuson. The English version of this book, which I wrote in German, owes much to the expert advice of my dear wife Mollie, the Manager of Peters Translation Service.

Bibliography

MEW: *Marx Engels Werke*, Institut für Marxismus-Leninismus beim ZK der SED (Berlin 1961).

MEGA: *Marx Engels Gesamtausgabe*, Abteilung III, Vol. 1 (Berlin 1975); Vol. 2 (Berlin 1979); Vol. 3 (Berlin 1981).

IISG: *Internationaal Instituut voor Sociale Geschiedenis*, Amsterdam.

Andréas, Bert, 'Marx' Verhaftung und Ausweisung, Brüssel, Februar/März 1848', in *Schriften aus dem Karl Marx-Haus, Trier,* 22.

Archiv für Sozialgeschichte, 2 Vols. (Hanover 1962).

Ball, Hugo, *Zur Kritik der deutschen Intelligenz* (Frankfurt 1980).

Born, Stephan, *Erinnerungen eines Achtundvierzigers* (Leipzig 1928 and Berlin/Bonn 1978).

Büttner, Wolfgang, *Georg Herwegh – ein Sänger des Proletariats* (Berlin 1886).

Der Bund der Kommunisten, Dokumente und Materialien, Vol. 1 (Berlin 1970).

Dornemann, Luise, *Jenny Marx. Der Lebensweg einer Sozialistin* (Berlin 1969).

Freiligrath, Ferdinand, *Gedichte* (Stuttgart 1964).

Häckel, Manfred, *Freiligraths Briefwechsel mit Marx und Engels* (Berlin, 1968).

Heine, Heinrich, *Sämtliche Schriften,* ed. Klaus Briegleb (Munich 1974).

Kapp, Ivonne, *Eleanor Marx* (New York 1972).

Karl-Marx-Album (Berlin 1953).

Karl Marx in Berlin, ed. Sepp Miller and Bruno Sawadzki (Berlin 1953).

Krosigk, Lutz Graf Schwerin v., *Jenny Marx – Liebe und Leid im Schatten von Karl Marx* (Wuppertal 1975).

Mayer, Gustav, 'Neue Beiträge zur Biographie von Karl Marx', in *Archiv für die Geschichte des Sozialismus und der Arbeiterbewegung*, 10 (Leipzig 1922).

Mohr und General. Erinnerungen an Marx und Engels (Berlin 1965).

Monz, Heinz, *Karl Marx. Grundlagen der Entwicklung zu Leben und Werk* (Trier 1973).

Nicolajewsky, Boris and Otto Maenchen-Helfen, *Karl Marx: Man and Fighter* (London 1976).

Padover, Saul, *Karl Marx. An Intimate Biography* (New York 1978).

Payne, Robert, *Marx. A Biography* (New York 1968).

Raddatz, Fritz J., *Karl Marx. Eine politische Biographie* (Hamburg 1975).

Ruge, Arnold, *Briefwechsel und Tagebuchblätter aus den Jahren 1825–1880,* ed. Paul Nerrlich (Berlin 1886).

Shakespeare Jahrbuch, Vol. 105 (1969).

Stieber, Wilhelm, *Spion des Kanzlers* (Munich 1981).

Die Töchter von Karl Marx, Unveröffentlichte Briefe (Cologne 1981).

Vogt, K(C)arl, *Mein Prozeß gegen die Allgemeine Zeitung* (Genf 1859).

Notes

Introduction

1. MEGA III, 1, p. 337.
2. Kapp, p. 298.

1. *Rebellious Blood*

1. MEW XIV, p. 433.
2. Krosigk, p. 175.

2. *A Childhood in Trier*

1. Krosigk, p. 183.
2. Ibid., p. 15.
3. Raddatz, p. 36.
4. Krosigk, p. 17.
5. Goethe, *Faust* Part II, Act V.
6. MEGA I, 1, p. 12.
7. Ibid.
8. Ibid.

3. *Loving a Wild Boar*

1. MEGA III, 1, p. 289.
2. Ibid., p. 290.
3. Ibid., p. 296.
4. Ibid., p. 303.
5. Ibid., p. 304.
6. Ibid., p. 306.
7. Ibid.
8. Ibid., p. 9 f.
9. Ibid., p. 304.
10. Ibid., I, 1 (2), p. 661.
11. Payne, p. 71.

12. MEGA III, 1, p. 337.
13. Ibid., I, 1 (2), p. 607.
14. Ibid., III, 1, p. 331.
15. Ibid.
16. Ibid., p. 308.
17. Ibid.
18. Ibid., p. 338.
19. Krosigk, p. 41.
20. MEGA III, 1, p. 397.
21. Ibid., p. 366.
22. Ibid., p. 368.
23. *Karl Marx in Berlin*, p. 75.
24. MEW III, p. 535.
25. MEGA I, 1 (2), p. 260.
26. Ibid., III, 1, p. 364.
27. Ibid., p. 368.
28. Ibid., p. 28.
29. MEW I, p. 54.
30. MEGA III, 1, p. 338.

4. *A Bookworm's Honeymoon*

1. MEGA III, 1, p. 38.
2. Ibid., p. 33.
3. Ibid.
4. Ibid.
5. Ibid.
6. Ibid., p. 396.
7. Ibid.
8. Ibid., p. 397.
9. Goethe, *Torquato Tasso*, II. 1.
10. MEGA I, 1, p. 152 f.
11. Ibid., I, 1, p. 366.
12. Ibid., III, 1, p. 396.
13. Ibid., p. 47.
14. Ibid., p. 44.
15. Ibid., p. 45.
16. Ibid., p. 397.
17. MEGA I, 2, p. 311.
18. Ibid.
19. MEW I, p. 372.
20. Nicolajewsky, p. 68.

5. *The Clarion Call of the Gallic Cock*

1. MEW I, p. 391.

2. MEGA III, 1, p. 412.
3. Nicolajewsky, p. 77.
4. Büttner, p. 45.
5. Ibid., p. 47.
6. Ibid.
7. Ibid., p. 50.
8. Ibid., p. 49.
9. Nicolajewsky, p. 68.
10. Büttner, p. 72.
11. Ruge, I. 349.
12. Nicolajewsky, p. 125.
13. Heine, II. 103.
14. Ibid., V. 232.
15. Ibid.
16. *Mohr*, p. 205.
17. MEGA III, 1, p. 442.
18. *Mohr*, p. 205.
19. MEGA III, 1, p. 440.
20. Ibid.
21. Ibid., p. 429.
22. Ibid., p. 429 f.
23. Ibid., p. 439.
24. Ibid.
25. Ibid.
26. MEW I, p. 391.
27. MEGA III, 1, p. 443.
28. Ibid., p. 442.
29. Ibid.
30. Ibid.
31. Ibid., p. 441.
32. MEW I, p. 405.
33. MEGA III, 1, p. 244.
34. *Mohr*, p. 205.
35. MEGA III, 1, p. 453.
36. *Mohr*, p. 205.

6. *Exile in Brussels*

1. Krosigk, p. 59.
2. Born, p. 39.
3. *Mohr*, p. 216.
4. MEGA III, 1, p. 263.
5. Freiligrath, p. 43.
6. Ibid., p. 115.
7. Häckel, I, p. 30.
8. Ibid., p. 116.
9. MEGA III, 1, p. 479.

10. MEGA III, 1, p. 263.
11. Ibid., p. 480.
12. Born, p. 41.
13. *Mohr*, p. 109.
14. MEW III, p. 35.
15. MEGA III, 1, p. 517.
16. Ibid., p. 518.
17. Ibid., p. 519.
18. Padover, p. 112.
19. MEGA III, 2, p. 10.
20. Ibid., p. 20.
21. Ibid., p. 16.
22. IISG, Brussels 1847–8.
23. MEGA III, 2, p. 219.
24. Ibid., p. 253.
25. Ibid., p. 125.
26. Ibid.
27. *Deutsche Brüsseler Zeitung,* 9 Dec. 1847.
28. Ibid., 6 Jan. 1848.
29. *Mohr*, p. 207.
30. IISG, Feb. 1848.
31. MEW IV, p. 530.
32. MEGA III, 2, p. 389.
33. *Mohr*, p. 208.
34. Ibid.
35. Ibid., p. 209.
36. Ibid.
37. Born, p. 49.

7.   *The Year of Decision 1848–1849*

1. Andreas, p. 54.
2. MEGA III, 2, p. 564.
3. Ibid.
4. Ibid., p. 143.
5. Ibid., 1, p. 518.
6. Ibid., 2, p. 422.
7. Ibid., p. 414.
8. MEGA III, 2, p. 152.
9. Ibid., p. 162.
10. *Bund der Kommunisten*, p. 849.
11. MEGA III, 2, p. 168.
12. *Bund der Kommunisten*, p. 84.
13. Ibid., p. 895.
14. MEW VI, p. 241.
15. Ibid., p. 480.
16. Ibid., p. 503.

17. *Karl-Marx-Album*, p. 92.
18. MEGA III, 3, p. 125.
19. Ibid.
20. Ibid.
21. IISG, Paris, 14 July 1849.
22. *Mohr*, p. 210.

8.   *The Hells of London*

1. *Mohr*, p. 240.
2. Ibid., p. 240 f.
3. Ibid., p. 214.
4. Ibid., p. 212.
5. Payne, p. 235.
6. MEW VI, p. 316.
7. Mayer, p. 62 f.
8. Ibid., p. 58.
9. *Mohr*, p. 214.
10. MEGA III, 3, p. 621 f.
11. Ibid.
12. Ibid.
13. *Mohr*, p. 215.

9.   *Death Street*

1. Mayer, p. 58.
2. MEW XXX, p. 248.
3. MEGA III, 3, p. 99.
4. Ibid., p. 108.
5. *Mohr*, p. 216.
6. Ibid.
7. Born, p. 39.
8. *Mohr*, p. 109.
9. MEW XXVIII, p. 85.
10. Ibid., p. 490.
11. Ibid.
12. *Mohr*, p. 217.
13. Ibid.
14. Stieber, p. 32.
15. Ibid., p. 30.
16. Ibid., p. 33.
17. Ibid.
18. MEW XXVIII, p. 641.
19. Ibid., p. 642.
20. Ibid., p. 128.
21. Ibid.

22. *Mohr*, p. 220.
23. Ibid.
24. Ibid.
25. MEW XXVIII, p. 370.
26. Ibid., p. 371.
27. Ibid., p. 423.
28. *Mohr*, p. 244.
29. MEW XXVIII, p. 441.
30. Ibid., p. 442.
31. Ibid., p. 444.
32. IISG, Jenny to Lassalle, April 1861.
33. MEW XXVIII, p. 415.
34. 28 June 1855.
35. MEW XXVIII, p. 438.
36. Ibid.
37. Archiv II, p. 176.
38. MEW XXX, p. 671.
39. Ibid., XXIX, p. 40.
40. Ibid., p. 532.
41. Ibid.
42. IISG, F132.
43. Ibid.
44. Ibid.
45. Ibid.
46. MEW XXIX, p. 67.
47. Ibid.
48. Archiv, p. 177.
49. Ibid.

10. *At the Edge of the Abyss*

1. *Mohr*, p. 113.
2. Krosigk, p. 97.
3. Ibid.
4. Ibid., p. 98.
5. *Mohr*, p. 222.
6. Ibid., p. 221.
7. Ibid.
8. MEW XXIX, p. 150.
9. Ibid., p. 151.
10. Ibid., p. 156.
11. Ibid., p. 267.
12. Ibid., p. 343.
13. Ibid., p. 344.
14. Ibid., p. 345.
15. Krosigk, p. 103.
16. MEW XXIX, p. 374.

17. MEW XXIX, p. 374.
18. Ibid., XXIX, p. 385.
19. Ibid., p. 442.
20. Ibid., p. 653.
21. Ibid., XXX, p. 8.
22. Ibid., p. 11.
23. Ibid.
24. Ibid., XXIX, p. 654.
25. Ibid., XXX, p. 683.
26. Ibid.
27. Ibid., p. 38.
28. Ibid., p. 85.
29. Vogt, p. 151 f.
30. MEW XXX, p. 683.
31. *Mohr*, p. 256.
32. Ibid., p. 257.
33. Ibid., p. 258.
34. Ibid.
35. Ibid., p. 259.
36. MEW XXX, p. 159.
37. Ibid., p. 168.
38. Ibid., p. 590.
39. IISG, Feb. 1861.
40. Ibid., April 1861.
41. MEW XXX, p. 603.
42. Ibid., p. 601.
43. Ibid., p. 602.
44. IISG, April 1861.
45. *Mohr*, p. 228.
46. IISG, April 1861.
47. Ibid.
48. Ibid.
49. MEW XXX, p. 248.
50. Ibid.
51. *Mohr*, p. 235.
52. MEW XXX, p. 257.
53. Ibid.
54. Ibid., p. 280.
55. *Mohr*, p. 229.
56. MEW XXX, p. 303.
57. Ibid.
58. Ibid., p. 309.
59. Ibid., p. 312.
60. Ibid., p. 314.
61. Ibid., p. 315.
62. Ibid., p. 318.
63. Ibid., p. 324.
64. Ibid.

65. MEW XXX, p. 324.
66. Ibid., p. 342.
67. Ibid., p. 347.
68. Ibid., p. 691.
69. *Mohr*, p. 230.
70. MEW XXX, p. 376.
71. Ibid.
72. Ibid., p. 380.
73. Ibid., p. 382.
74. IISG, D3309, Dec.–Jan. 1863–4.
75. *Mohr*, p. 231.

11.   *Politics as Fate*

1. Archiv, p. 177.
2. Ibid., p. 178.
3. Ibid., p. 179.
4. MEW XXXIII, p. 703.
5. Archiv, p. 182.
6. MEW XXX, p. 665.
7. Payne, p. 355.
8. *Mohr*, p. 232.
9. MEW XXXI, p. 417.
10. Ibid.
11. Ibid., p. 10.
12. Ibid., p. 591.
13. IISG, Jenny to Frau Liebknecht, 16 May 1865.
14. Ibid.
15. Ibid.
16. Ibid.
17. MEW XXXI, p. 133.
18. Ibid., p. 123.
19. Ibid., p. 139.
20. Ibid., p. 140.
21. Ibid., p. 583.
22. Ibid., p. 342.
23. Ibid., p. 151.
24. Ibid.
25. *Die Töchter*, p. 6.
26. Ibid., p. 30.
27. Ibid.
28. MEW XXXI, p. 593.
29. Kapp, p. 298.
30. Ibid., p. 74.
31. Ibid.
32. MEW XXXII, p. 692.
33. Ibid.

34. MEW XXXI, p. 227.
35. Ibid.
36. Ibid., XVI, p. 549.
37. Ibid., XXXI, p. 262.
38. Ibid., XXXII, p. 217.
39. Ibid., XVI, p. 510.
40. Ibid.
41. Ibid.
42. Ibid., p. 511.
43. Ibid., p. 439.
44. Ibid., p. 579.
45. Ibid., p. 581.
46. Ibid., XXXII, p. 703.
47. Ibid.
48. Ibid., XXXI, p. 290.
49. Ibid.
50. Ibid., p. 595.
51. Ibid.
52. Ibid., XXII, p. 533.
53. Ibid., p. 686.
54. Ibid., p. 705.
55. Ibid.
56. Ibid.
57. Ibid., p. 714.
58. Ibid.
59. Ibid.
60. Ibid., XXXI, p. 290.
61. Ibid., XXXIII, p. 675.
62. Ibid.
63. Ibid., XVII, p. 6.
64. Ibid., p. 362.
65. Ibid.
66. Ibid.
67. Ibid., XXXIII, p. 238.
68. Ibid., p. 686.
69. Ibid., XVII, p. 371.
70. Ibid., p. 366.
71. Ibid., XXXIII, p. 681.
72. Archiv, p. 245.
73. Ball, p. 204.
74. MEW XVIII, p. 22.
75. Ibid., XXXIII, p. 702.
76. Ibid.

12. *Retired Revolutionaries*

1. MEW XXXIII, p. 505.

2. *Mohr*, p. 310.
3. Ibid., p. 311.
4. Ibid., p. 312.
5. Kapp, p. 153.
6. MEW XXXIII, p. 703.
7. *Die Töchter*, p. 159.
8. *Mohr*, p. 288.
9. Ibid.
10. MEW XXXIV, p. 52.
11. *Shakespeare J*, CV, p. 55.
12. Ibid., p. 65.
13. Ibid., p. 66.
14. *Mohr*, p. 347.

Postscript

1. MEW XXXV, p. 248.
2. Ibid., p. 249.
3. Ibid., p. 242.

Index

3 1221 03314 9522

PROPERTY OF
EDMONTON PUBLIC LIBRARY

NiC